This book is dedicated to Skyla.

When the time comes you will know how hard Daddy fought for you.

Contents

All of my life I have suffered with acute shyness, finding it extremely difficult to express my thoughts and communicate my feelings.

2020, a year to remember in many ways, has been the most stressful year to date, not just for myself, but for my family who have supported me throughout.

Writing this memoir, and finally putting my thoughts onto paper, I hope will serve as not only a reminder of the events and how they unfolded, but also, as 'therapy', a way to find some closure, and sheer determination to show others who have doubted my ability to write this story, that 'I am here'. You can do anything with the drive and the motivation to do so!

The biggest and most important reason for doing this, is Skyla. My world, my everything, and without whom none of this would have happened. While I will always regret the events that unfolded in 2019 and 2020, I will never regret my little girl. My hope, when she reads this in years to come, she will know how hard I had to fight for my baby girl and the devotion I have for her. Above all, she will know that my love for her has never faltered. She has my heart. From the moment she entered this world, to now, and for always. While others have tried to prise her away from me, we will always have an unbreakable bond. This is our truth.

Finding Myself

Let's start from the beginning...

Life before Skyla was normal, and after it completely extraordinary. If you feel compelled to know more, stick with me and I will tell you our story......

The year was 2017, and I had recently moved back in with my parents after a relationship break up. At this time, I was feeling pretty low. Hollie was my first love, and the end of our relationship was hard. Looking back, I realised that we were both so young when we set up home together, and after three years, we simply drifted apart. The hardest thing was moving home, having been independent for a while.

I had become quite complacent living with Hollie, and had piled on the pounds, knocking my confidence and my ability to engage with people face to face. I had never been confident, especially with girls, and felt unattractive, not liking how I looked or felt when I looked in the mirror.

I threw myself into work, as a shop assistant at a retail store in Cirencester and joined a local gym. This helped to give myself focus and take my mind off my failed relationship. It also helped to make me feel better about myself, and I started to like me, and how I looked.

Slowly but surely, the pounds started dropping and the muscle started building. I gained quite a bit of confidence and I was reasonably happy with my life. It was quiet and steady, and whilst I will never be the life and soul of the party, I was content with that. The only thing missing was somebody to love and that is something I have always craved.

I was working full time with odd hours, so when I wasn't working or at the gym, I spent time with my friends, and like most guys of my generation, a disproportionate amount of time with my face glued to social media.

I am a huge lover of music, but more than the melody, I love listening to lyrics. I will hear the words of a song and it will just be EXACTLY what I want to say but had no way of saying it myself. Using the medium of Facebook has been instrumental in being able to express my emotion of that time, using music videos as a platform.

On those nights when led in bed, like so many others, I would spend my time scrolling through Facebook and reading posts from 'friends'. I say friends in quotations, because as you know, the vast majority of people you are 'friends' with on Facebook are nothing more than mere acquaintances. I must confess, like so many others, to accepting some friend requests from people I've never even bloody heard of, but hey, Facebook friend numbers are great aren't they!

This is what it was like with Ann. I did know OF Ann, having gone to the same secondary school as her, but I wouldn't say that I KNEW her, but nevertheless, she became one of my Facebook friends.

Looking back, I suppose you could say that this story starts with one Facebook post that I should never have responded to, but I did. I was just finishing up at the gym and taking my obligatory 'post-workout' selfie and feeling pretty good about the progress I was making with my fitness. I started my usual scrolling through my newsfeed when Ann's post caught my eye. Very simply it said, "Feeling lonely and sad". I felt a bit sorry for her as her previous Facebook posts had been consistent with a single Mother who was clearly going through a tough time.

And there it was! That moment when I 'slid into her DM's'. I quickly typed out a message "Well I'm free if you want to talk and have a catch up".

She responded quickly with her address, and I did a quick search and was pleased to see that it wasn't far out of my way on my walk home, so I let her know I would drop by in about half an hour.

She was living in a new build not far from my grandmother's house and as she directed me to take a seat in the living room, I noted that everything looked new. She told me that she hadn't long lived there, having been moved by the Housing Association from a locally notorious, recently condemned block of flats close to my home.

She told me how happy she was to have been moved and how lucky she felt to have been given a brand-new house such as this. I could tell from the way she was almost bragging that she was more than a little bit proud of the game she played with the housing association, making it seem as though she hadn't really wanted to leave Patterson Road and thus pushing them to offer her £10,000 to do so.

If I'm honest, I didn't really see anything wrong in this at the time. I just thought she was a 'savvy' Mum trying to do the best she could on what little she had.

Ann went to make me a coffee and I sat on her sofa and looked around the room. The walls were decorated with quite a few photos of Ann and two young children. The living room was clean and tidy but definite signs of small children in residence, with toys stacked up in a corner.

The next couple of hours passed quite quickly as Ann told me all about her children, Tiffany and Tammie who were sleeping upstairs. Tiffany was three and Tammie just a baby. I was happy to sit and listen while she told me all about the toxic relationship, she had endured with the kids Father. She was quite tearful explaining that she had fallen in love with him and had dreamed of their wedding and bringing up their two beautiful kids together.

She told me how she had fought to keep the relationship going but that he had become more and more controlling. Not wanting her to go out and meet friends or do anything with the kids without him, and constantly yelling. She hated the yelling. Especially in front of the children. She sadly told me that things had come to a head when he had turned violent and pushed her violently while she was holding the baby. It was then she realised that things were never going to work and how she had threatened to call the police if he didn't leave.

Once he was out of the house, he started a campaign of vile and threatening messages on social media and text messages to the point that she felt that she had no choice but to apply for a restraining order, ensuring the safety of both herself and the children.

It was because of this, she told me, that she felt so lonely. Recently she had only left the house to take Tiffany to Playgroup or to visit her Mum as she was scared he might be watching.

I felt so sorry for her. She was clearly a loving mother who was trying to pick up the pieces of her life after her relationship had broken down and was missing having 'adult' conversation. It was hard for her.

It got to about 11 o'clock at night and I told her that I had to go home as I had to work the next day but asked if I could see her again. I'll be honest, I was a little bit wary, as her family was quite well-known in Cirencester for all the wrong reasons, but as far as I knew, Ann had never been in any trouble, and I liked her. I was relieved when she nodded shyly, and I gave her a bit of a hug as I was leaving.

As I walked home, I couldn't help feeling angry at her ex, Mike. How could he? He had everything. A loving girlfriend and 2 beautiful Daughters. It was all I ever really dreamed of. That kind of happy family unit. How on earth could he behave violently like that? Especially while she was holding such a tiny, fragile baby.

Over the next 24 hours we exchanged dozens of private messages and she invited me over after work a day or two later. I had worked the early shift, so I quickly agreed. I couldn't help feeling a little excited but vowed to myself to take things slowly. She had only just split up with Mike and I didn't want to be a rebound, and if I'm honest, for the first time in my life I was starting to feel comfortable being single.

That afternoon I arrived at her door, and it was quickly opened. Ann had a baby in her arms and a little girl just peeping out from behind her legs. This was my first encounter with Tiffany and Tammie. Tammie was just a baby at the time, so I didn't really have much interaction with her for the first few meetings, but Tiffany's initial shyness was soon taken over by her natural high energy. She spent most of that afternoon chattering away and insisting on showing me things and inviting me to play.

I felt really comfortable with Ann, and we continued to chat away about what we had been up to since school. As I have explained before, I am naturally very quiet and shy, but I found it easy to chat to Ann. I won't say that I told her my life story at this stage, I didn't, but I was enjoying her company.

As a single Mum, I had imagined that it wouldn't be easy to see Ann outside of her home, but she was fortunate that her Mum loved having the kids and would take every opportunity to have them to stay which meant that we would quite often meet each other in the local pubs.

None of these meetings were 'dates' as such. I would be out with my friends, and she would be out with hers and nine times out of ten I would end up going home with her. At this stage everything was quite casual, which is the way I liked it.

I wasn't sure how I felt about the whole situation. I was really quite confused; I did like Ann, but I didn't want to get too close in case I got hurt again and I was happy with our casual arrangement.

I pretty much kept our relationship a secret at this stage. I didn't know what we were or where we might be going, if anywhere, so saw little point in telling anyone about it. Besides, it was private.

We settled into a casual sort of routine. I would drop by after work, bringing some toys or treats for the kids and we did things that most young couples do in a causal relationship. But besides that, we did talk a lot.

As I mentioned before, Ann came from a 'rough' family and was known by a different surname at school. She explained that she had changed her name to her mother's maiden name to try to shake off that reputation. Her brothers were well known in Cirencester for being local thugs and general troublemakers and had both dabbled in drugs. It wasn't anything too serious but what my family would just call 'rough'. I was impressed that she had felt strongly enough to do that. It couldn't be easy having a 'reputation' for something that you had no part in, but she had done everything she could to make sure she wasn't seen as just a 'Thomas'. 'Fair play,' I thought.

She was really close to her Mum, Lynne, and because she spent a lot of time with her, I met her quite early on. She was friendly and welcoming. The only fly in the ointment of their relationship was that Lynne had really liked Mike and she still pushed for Ann to ignore the Restraining Order and allow Mike to have contact with the kids, but, for the most part, they just agreed to disagree and got on with almost raising the girls together.

It was a comfortable set up, but because it was 'comfortable' I started to get 'uncomfortable'. It was a very gradual transition, but very slowly Ann started questioning what I was doing, where I was, where I was going, etc. Looking back, I suppose it was natural. If you spend enough time with someone, despite not putting a label on it, you kind of get into that routine and start expecting things to happen in a certain way.

When things start to trouble or worry me, I tend to withdraw into myself. My issue of not being able to express myself clearly and instead saying nothing and having it perceived as being moody first showed itself to Ann when she started to refer to me as 'Daddy' to Tiffany. I really wasn't comfortable with it and for many reasons.

One of them being that I really didn't want a serious relationship at this stage and was happy with the casual nature of what we had. Having her children call me Daddy put way too much pressure on me to make this relationship exactly that. A relationship. But more importantly, I wasn't Tiffany or Tammie's Daddy. Don't get me wrong, I was beginning to form a solid bond with them. I absolutely adored them, but it just didn't sit right with me.

My previous relationship had ended with my heart breaking after my ex-partner had aborted my baby. It destroyed me and I couldn't help looking at Tammie and wondering what my own baby would be like. How would it feel to hold my own baby in my arms and having her curl her little fingers into my beard? I felt broken just thinking about it and I was determined never to hurt like that again. I wanted to protect my heart at all costs.

It was for this reason that I started to pull away and not see so much of Ann. It made me a little sad, but I thought it was for the best. I didn't want to hurt her feelings, so I just told Ann that I wasn't ready to handle having a baby that wasn't mine and so we separated on good terms. We would still exchange the odd comment on Facebook, but the messaging stopped, and I stopped dropping round after work. And that was that.

Christmas 2017 came and went, and life continued into 2018 with a monotonous routine. Work, gym, sleep, repeat. My work hours were quite erratic, so weekend nights out were a rare occurrence, but when they happened, I tended to meet with friends or go out with my brother and Dad for a few beers.

All in all, I was content. I wouldn't say I was blissfully happy. I still longed for a partner to share my life with, but I was also enjoying searching for the "one" the way young blokes do!

In around January 2018 I bumped into Ann again at the local nightclub. We started our usual flirting and I ended up going home with her. It just felt natural and when I woke up the next morning it didn't feel awkward at all.

We stayed in bed for much of the morning just chatting about what we had been up to.

"I missed you," she said quietly. It was probably at that moment that I realised that I had missed her too. I remained quiet for a while with my arms wrapped around her while 100 thoughts ran through my head. I could have it all. I just had to allow myself to be happy and embrace this ready-made family that was right there on offer.

"Me too," I replied just as quietly. "Can we start again?" I asked. She answered with a smile.

From that moment we became a couple. I still wasn't ready to share my news with the wider world. I'm not sure why. I have always worried about what people think and I knew that most people, especially my parents, would have an opinion about the fact that Ann was a single Mother of two kids. Added to which her family history was bound to be a concern. So, I kept it to myself, and I enjoyed the secrecy of it.

I saw Ann as often as I could and started allowing myself to bond with Tiffany and Tammie. Tammie was growing up fast. She was a year old now and crawling and Tiffany was bright as a button. I loved playing with them both and relished every minute that we spent together as a 'family'. As I spent more and more nights away from my parents' house, my whole family were constantly teasing me wanting to know who I was seeing, and I enjoyed the tease of keeping tight-lipped.

"When are we going to meet this mystery girl?" my Mum would ask for the millionth time as I prepared my protein shake. I would just smile and shrug my shoulders. She would just shake her head, but I could tell that she was happy that I was looking so happy.

At the beginning of June of 2018 things had become a little strained between Ann and me. She was constantly wanting to know where I was and when I was coming round, but when we were together, she was moody and snappy. "What's wrong?" I asked over and over. "Nothing," or "I don't feel very well," was the usual response. I couldn't understand it and it was starting to get on my nerves.

One evening I was changing Tammie's nappy on the living room floor when I looked over at Ann who looked almost green. "Are you OK?" I asked her, concerned. She just nodded and stared miserably at the TV.
"I reckon you're pregnant!" I said it the minute the thought entered my head, it suddenly made perfect sense. The sudden mood swings, the constant tiredness that she had been suffering from.

"Don't be stupid," she snapped. "I'm on the pill." She was looking at me as though I was mad, but I felt sure it was a reasonable assumption.
"When was your last, you know, period?"
"Shut up and stop being stupid," she said.
I shook my head and carried on with the nappy change. Picking Tammie up and swinging her up into my arms, I couldn't help feeling a little spark of excitement and terror all at same time.

Could she be? Was she? God, I was happy with her, and I really did love both Ann and the girls, but a baby of our own?

I was due to start work early the next morning and so I was going home to sleep so that I was closer to work and also so that I didn't disturb any of them when I got up at the crack of dawn. I didn't want to leave with this hanging in the air, so I closed the topic with a "well if you're sure."

"I am," she said, "It's not possible, I've just got a bug or something."

I didn't sleep at all that night. The idea just kept going over and over in my head. What if she really was pregnant? How did I feel about it? Of course, I knew how I felt about it. Excited beyond belief, but how would SHE feel about it? She already had two small children and she was clearly not planning a third right now. Of course, I had told her how I longed for a child myself, but not right now. Our relationship was still in the very early stages, and I still hadn't felt comfortable enough to 'go public', so I suppose, in the back of my mind, I just wasn't thinking about a long-term future at that point. I was living in the now. I was sure that Ann felt the same way too. Although we had both told each other that we wouldn't be 'seeing' other people and that we were exclusive, she also hadn't introduced me to her wider family or updated her status on social media. Although it wasn't something we spoke about, I felt that she was also happy just getting to know each other without any of the pressures of outside influences.

I was conscious of getting ahead of myself. Was I thinking this because it was what I really wanted? So many confusing thoughts were running through my head. I decided to trust Ann. After all, she had been pregnant twice before so she would surely know if she was pregnant again. Was I disappointed? Relieved at the prospect that my gut feeling was way off? I don't know. Probably a bit of both.

I carried on working, seeing Ann and going home to my parents for the next few nights until a few days later when I was at work and for whatever reason I pulled a pregnancy testing kit from the shelf I was stacking. I stood there looking at it and wondering. There was nothing else for it. I was going to get no peace from my own thoughts until I knew for sure, so after my shift I paid for a kit and put it in my bag.

That afternoon I went round to Ann's as usual. She had still been feeling under the weather but told me that she had been feeling a little better, although still very tired. I didn't say anything about the pregnancy test at that point, simply offered to make tea for the whole family which she accepted gratefully.

I prepared Tammie's baby food and some chicken nuggets for Tiffany and threw together a lasagne for myself and Ann. I was feeling nervous, wondering how to broach the subject again. We put the kids to bed, and I went to my bag and pulled out the kit. She looked at me with a puzzled expression. "What's that for?" She asked as I held it out to her.

"Uh, well that's a stupid question," I laughed nervously.

"I already told you, I'm on the pill," she said. But she didn't look angry.

"But don't you think you might be?"

She looked at the floor.

"I don't see how I can be, but what if I am? What are we going to do?"

Oh God! What did she mean? Did she mean if she was, she might want to get rid of it? The thought horrified me. Not again, I thought with despair. "Please Ann," I said, "Just take the test and then we will know, and if you aren't then you need to go and see a doctor, because you aren't well."

She looked relieved at that response. Almost as though she had been worried that I didn't believe that she had been feeling so poorly.

"I'll do it tomorrow," she said, "you have to do them in the morning to get the best result."

"But I won't be here," I fretted, "I want to be here." I had to start work in the early hours again, so had no choice but to go home.

"Don't be silly," Ann said, "the result won't change whether you are here or not, and we have to do it properly."

And so, another sleepless night was had.

I started work at 6:00am. Before going onto the shop floor, I kept checking my phone, but nothing. I had to leave my phone in my locker and the next three hours passed so slowly. Had she taken the test yet? What was the result? I couldn't wait for my break.

Break time came and I couldn't wait to check my phone for messages. There were a couple of alerts from friends, but there in my PM's was one from Ann. Nervously I opened it. It was just a picture. Of a pregnancy test. It took me a minute to decipher the two lines. I think I stopped breathing. I pinched the screen to enlarge the image so that the two lines in the windows filled the screen and just stared. And in that moment, I knew exactly how I felt. Tears filled my eyes with happiness. I'm not a bloke of many words at the best of times, but there was no way of putting into words my joy at that moment.

Quickly I typed out a reply message letting her know I would be coming to her house straight after work.

The rest of my shift passed so slowly. At times I was convinced that the clocks had stopped altogether. All sorts of thoughts were whizzing through my head. "Oh my God, I'm going to be a dad"!" Then horror as the next thought of "What if she doesn't want to keep it?" I felt sick with nervous excitement, until at last, it was time to grab my coat and walk as fast as I could to Ann's house. I think I covered the mile and a half in about 15 minutes flat as I had broken into almost a run in places.

I arrived at the front door and gave a sharp tap on the wood with my knuckles. Ann opened the door and looked really nervous, I stepped in and just grinned at her. "Are you OK about it?" She asked.
I smiled and nodded.
She visibly sighed with relief and then flung her arms around me laughing.
"Shit," she said "Three kids under 5! How the hell am I going to cope?"
"You won't be on your own this time," I promised. "I will be here every step of the way".

And with that, I was going to be a dad. Things moved quickly from there. We were yet to announce to the world our news. After all, very few people even knew we had been seeing each other, so this was going to come as a huge shock. I knew that people were going to think it was moving too fast, but I didn't really care. I was getting my happily ever after and nobody was going to spoil it for me.

The first thing to do was to introduce Ann to my family as my girlfriend. Of course, they already knew I had been seeing someone, but because I had been so secretive, they knew next to nothing about Ann. I started to drop a bit more information as to where I was going when I went round to see Ann and dropping her into conversation.

Everybody seemed to be interested in the details. Ashley and Jade already kind of knew her. Cirencester is so small that when you are in the same generation, everyone knows everyone, or at the very least knows someone who knows someone! Both Ash and Jade raised the topic of her family and I responded quite curtly with "Well that's her brothers – not her!"
And they backed off. Jade was living with us by now as they saved for a deposit on their own place, so I'd gotten to know Jade quite well.

Over the next few weeks I spent more and more time with Amy and her Mum together with the girls. I knew that Ann was incredibly close to her, so I was keen to get on well with her. As I spent more time with her she seemed to accept me as part of the family.

We still hadn't told anyone about the baby. We wanted to get to the first scan, as normal couples do, but it also didn't feel right to announce to Mum and Dad that they were going to be Grandparents when they hadn't even met the mother of my baby yet so I choreographed a careful plan to try and get things in the right order, but as quickly as I could.

I arranged for Ann and the girls to come round to a family barbecue. Mum adores kids (it's probably where I get my love of children from) and has a natural affinity to them, so she was more than welcoming. My Dad is also really easy-going and while he might not totally trust everything at face-value he usually gives everyone the benefit of the doubt. It was a relaxed afternoon for the kids, but I could tell that Ann was feeling awkward. I think she felt like she was being interviewed so she was quite quiet.

I think she felt most intimidated by Jade. She knew that Jade was aware of her family's reputation, and I think it worried her that she was being judged. I told her not to let it bother her and it didn't really matter. Jade would soon get to know Ann for herself and then she would see that she really didn't follow in her family's footsteps.

Of course, there were the anticipated questions about Tiffany and Tammie's Father and Ann told them about the relationship she had shared with Mike and his violence. "Does he see the girls?" My Mum asked.

"No," Ann replied, "He's not allowed to." and quickly moved the conversation on.

Over the next few weeks, I included Ann in any family 'outings' that I went to. As a family we quite often went out for a drink or a meal on the weekends and these events now always included Ann and the girls. Mum was over the moon to have two small children to entertain and went out of her way to include them in our family. I could tell even Dad was getting quite close to Tiffany and Tammie and the girls certainly loved spending time with them – they got spoilt rotten.

The next step was to move in. I broke it to Mum and Dad over tea one evening. They were a bit shocked at the speed it was happening, but they understood that I had been seeing Ann for a lot longer than they had necessarily known about.

Again, Ann's background came up. "I heard that Mike. . ." Mum would start, but I would cut her off with

"It doesn't matter what you heard!" and she quickly understood that I didn't want to discuss it. Mike had shown no interest in the kids, and they were a part of MY family now and I would move heaven and earth to protect them, but I also understood that Mum and Dad were just trying to make sure that I knew what I was doing. I did. So, I packed up my stuff and moved in with Ann early July.

The person I was most nervous about introducing Ann to was Nan. She might be getting on a bit and is a tiny 4ft 10in, but she can be quite scary. She certainly doesn't hold back on her opinions and says things exactly as she sees them. A member of the PC Brigade she most certainly is not! But it was really important to me that she approved. I am really close to my nan. My grandad had been killed just 8 years earlier in a horrific car accident and the whole family had been devastated and we had all become extremely protective of Nan.

I asked Nan if she could drive me to Swindon as I had some errands to do. I just forgot to mention that Ann and the girls would be coming too. I gave Nan the address and when she pulled up outside, I went out to meet her with one of the kid's child seats. Nan looked a bit puzzled and I just shot her a cheeky smile and said, "you don't mind if Ann comes do you?"

Nan looked shocked, "I don't suppose I have much choice, do I?", she said sternly.

I laughed nervously and shook my head.

It was quite quiet on the drive to Swindon, and once we got there, I left them to it as I had an appointment at the Driving Test Centre. I did worry about how they were getting on, but luckily when we met up an hour later, I could see that even if Ann hadn't won Nan over yet, Tiffany certainly had.

Now we were just waiting for the right time to make the announcement. I was getting more and more excited. I had been to the first scan and had felt an overwhelming wave of love and excitement as I stared at the blob on the screen.

I couldn't wait to share my news with everyone, but I still wanted to handle it carefully. I couldn't keep it totally to myself and sent Ash a text message.

(Me) *Bro, got something to tell you.*
(Ash) *What?*
(Me) *I'm going to be a Dad.*
(Ash) *Congratulations!! I won't say anything. Beer SOOOON!*

I felt happier knowing that I had at least shared my secret with one person close to me and I knew he would be chuffed for me, but I was dreading telling everyone else as I really didn't know if they would be happy for me or not. I was almost certain everyone would think it was too soon and knew I needed to make the announcement soon, but things took a bit of an unexpected turn.

About a week after telling Ash, he suddenly announced to everyone that Jade was expecting their baby. I won't deny it. I was a bit pissed off. It was totally irrational, but I felt like they had only announced it to steal MY thunder. Why couldn't they have waited? They knew that Ann was pregnant, and I was upset that I had confided in Ash, but he hadn't done the same with me.

But while I was upset, Ann was livid. She was certain it was Jade that had pushed Ash to make the announcement so early. "She can't even be a month pregnant yet," she said.

"Well Ash said she was due late February," I pointed out "That's only a couple of weeks later than you".

"That's even worse!" She exclaimed "My baby is due first! WE should have announced it first".

However, I didn't really get the opportunity to ask why they hadn't told me first when they knew I was having a baby too, because all hell had broken loose over their news.

Dad was furious and Nan would not be held back over her opinion on the matter. The general opinion being that they were too young, not settled enough and without a proper home of their own. The fall-out just made me more nervous about telling them my own news, but it had to be done. Ann was beginning to show, and I had seen both Nan and Mum stare at her tummy more than a couple of times and I was sure they suspected.

"You have to tell them," Ann said. "I don't see why I should keep hiding it and I want to tell MY Mum. It's not all about YOUR family you know."

Of course, she was right. I was over the moon about becoming a dad and I just wanted my family to share that joy with me. The idea that I would receive a negative reaction was really hard to comprehend and I hoped against hope that there wouldn't be another fall out because of it...

A week had passed since Ash and Jade's bombshell and while nobody apart from Ash and Jade appeared to be over the moon about it, things had settled down.

"I will," I promised. "I'll do it this evening. We can go round after I finish work and tell them together".

She looked pleased at the idea. I can't say I wasn't nervous though. I really hoped they weren't going to react in the same way they had to Ash and Jade's news.

I already started practicing what I was going to say in retort to their objections.

"It's not up to you". "It's my life". "I'm an adult" were all options as I ran through various scenarios in my head. Only I didn't actually get the chance as it didn't play out at all like I had planned.

On my way to work I decided to give my Nan a ring. I wanted her to be the first to know. Sort of test out her reaction to give me an idea of the sort of reaction I could expect from everyone else. "You sitting down?" I asked.

"Why?"

I cleared my throat nervously "Ann's pregnant."

Silence. I waited. "Nan?"

"I heard you. Are you happy?"

"Yeah".

"Well then I'm happy for you" she said.

I breathed a sigh of relief. "I thought you might be angry with me like you are at Ash" I said.

"It's a bit different Carl," she said. "Ash is a lot younger than you and still living with his Mum and Dad. I'm not saying I think it's a great idea to have three children under the age of 5, but, well, as long as you are happy then I'm happy for you."

"Thanks Nan." I smiled. "Oh, don't mention it to Mum and Dad, me and Ann are going round this evening to tell them." She agreed and I hung up feeling a lot more positive.

I was heading home from work when my phone pinged. It was a message from my dad.

(Dad) *Not happy with you*
(Me) *Why????*

I tried to think what I could have done to make him cross but couldn't think of anything.

(Dad) Why you not tell us in person? Not happy she put it on Facebook.

The last message was punctuated with a sad face emoji.

Oh shit. I stopped in my tracks. Quickly I opened Facebook on my phone and scrolled through the notifications.

I had a shedload of "congratulations" messages. "Oh Crap, what has she done!!" I thought. I tapped in Ann's name into the search bar and up popped her profile. There it was. A picture of the two of us and the announcement of our baby due in February. Fuck! No wonder he wasn't happy with me. My phone pinged again.

(Dad) *She is out of order. Have you told Nan? I am happy for you xxx*

Shit that made it worse

I was reeling. Why on earth had Ann done this. We were supposed to do it together. And in person! I struggled to find the right words for a response.

(Me) Oh *No. I said not to put it on FB and I would have said a week ago, but Jade announced she was pregnant a few days after I told Ash.*
(Dad) *Still mean for you not to tell me in person. Ash is a different kettle f fish. Happy for you lad.*

Bloody hell – could he make me feel any more guilty. I quickened my pace to get home a bit quicker.

Opening the door, Ann was there on the sofa. She looked up from her phone. "You OK?".
"Not really, why did you put that on Facebook? Now my Mum and Dad are really upset with me."
She looked shocked. "What do you mean?" You told me you were telling them this morning, so I waited until lunch time and then posted it!"
"No! We were going to go and tell them together! Tonight! I said I was ringing to tell Nan this morning!"
"Oh Shit." she said looking guilty. "Sorry, I thought you said you were telling your Mum this morning."

I couldn't be angry; it was an honest mistake, and I was sure that Mum and Dad would forgive me once they realised that it was all a misunderstanding.

Once the cat was out of the bag, I felt like a huge weight had been lifted. I was happier than I think I had ever been. Tiffany and Tammie were the light of my life, and I was so excited at the thought of holding my new baby in my arms.

Christmas of 2017 approached, and Ann was now heavily pregnant. She was really struggling with hip and back pain, and I was doing my best to support her, but all in all life was good.

I needed to help Ann around the house and with the girls more and more as her pregnancy progressed, so my gym time was taking a bit of a back seat, but I didn't really mind. As Ann pointed out, I had responsibilities now and I was needed most at home.

We had decided to learn the sex of our baby. I think Ann had secretly hoped for a little boy as she already had two girls, but nevertheless we were both over the moon to discover that we were having another little girl.

We discussed names at length and couldn't agree on a first name until one day I saw the name Skyla somewhere. I committed it to memory and when I got home, I said, "I've found a name I like."
"Me too, she said."
And both at the same time we said.
"Skyla!"
We looked at each other in surprise and then started laughing. "That's it then," I said. But there was something that I had really wanted to speak to her about. The baby's middle name. If the baby had been a boy, I had really wanted to include Robert in his name as a nod to my granddad, but as I was having a little girl, I had another idea to honour him.
"Ann," I began "I wondered if you had any thoughts about a middle name?"
"Not really," she replied.
"Well, I would really like it to be Harris."
"Harris?"

"Yeah, after my grandads surname, I don't really want to call her Roberta, I laughed, but I really do want to have my grandad in there somewhere." I looked hopefully at her.

She looked thoughtful for a while and then looked up at me and said, "I like it."

Telling my Nan was incredible. When I announced what my baby's full name would be, she just welled up and then grabbed me for the biggest hug. "Don't cry Nan." I laughed.

"I'm just so happy. Your grandad would be so proud of you," she said wiping her eyes.

Just seeing my nan so happy was incredible for me. Apart from Ann being in pretty much constant pain at the moment, life couldn't be any better. And it would get even better as the birth of my baby would hopefully mean an end to Ann's pain and we could start our Happy Ever After right there.

Telling Lynne about the name wasn't as well received as it was by my own family. Of course, I hadn't expected it to be, as Harris was personal to just my side, but I had hoped that Lynne would like it.

"Harris?" She said. Her lip curling up as though she smelt something nasty. It was the first time Lynne had been overly critical of me or my ideas. I had witnessed how she sometimes spoke down to Ann, but overall, we had gotten on famously. Her Facebook feeds had been full of love and praise for the family that we had become. *"The best thing to ever happen to my daughter." "Carl is the best daddy to Tiffany and Tammie"* were just some of the comments that she made on family photos that I had uploaded to my Facebook timeline.

"Yes, it's after my grandad," I explained.

"I don't like it."

It stung a little, but I just shrugged and retorted "Oh well."

"I think you should have her middle name as Hannah. After Ann's nan as her due date is her nan's Birthday". She looked at Ann and Ann looked uncomfortable.

"Sorry Mum, but we've already decided she said quietly". Nothing more was said, but there was a definite change in the way she spoke to me from that point.

It was from then that Mike would be brought into the conversation more and more. It turned out that Lynne had been in regular contact with him. Ann even suspected that Lynne had been allowing him to see the girls when they stayed with her. There were times when Tiffany would come home and be quite secretive and started soiling herself. If we pressed her, she would clam up.

Ann was furious, but of course, Lynne denied it. Because, obviously, allowing Mike to see the kids would be a massive kick in the teeth for Ann. How on earth could a mother forgive the pain that he had caused her daughter. Not to mention the breach of the Restraining Order?

Still, we had no evidence, and it wasn't the time to cause problems over something that might not even be happening. Accusing her of such a thing would only cause a massive rift.

My first Christmas as a Family man, a 'Stepdad' and a 'Father to be' was fast approaching and I couldn't wait. I was definitely more excited than Tiffany. I had saved for months to buy a radio-controlled car that the girls could ride in that I knew that they would love along with dozens of smaller gifts. A lot of Tammie's gifts were educational toys focussing on speech as at close to two years old she hadn't yet said a single word. We were both a bit worried. It wasn't that she hadn't formed words yet, there was no attempt to do so. She remained silent. She cried and laughed with sound, but that was it. No other sounds at all, so I was determined to give her all the help I could.

I wasn't just focussing on the kids though. I was determined to enjoy this Christmas as a complete family. I had it all planned. Get up in the morning, watch the kids unwrap their gifts, exchange gifts with Ann and then I was going to prepare and serve a full traditional Christmas lunch for all of us. It was going to be perfect, and I couldn't wait.

Mum had been disappointed. This was going to be the first year that she hadn't had both her boys' round for Christmas dinner, but I think she understood how important this was to me.

I had to work on Christmas Eve and when I got home Lynne was there. As she was leaving, she said she was going to see Ann's Granddad on Christmas Day and then come round to give the girls their presents.
"That will be great" I said. "We are going to have our dinner at about 1, so if you come round after 3 or 4 that will be perfect".
Lynne said she couldn't wait and teased the girls that Santa wouldn't come if they didn't get to sleep by 9. We all laughed and as we said goodnight on the doorstep shouted, "Merry Christmas, see you at 4 tomorrow".
"Merry Christmas" she called back happily.

Putting the kids to bed that night was amazing. I really did have it all AND more to come. My happy little family. My dreams of a Christmas Eve where I created magic for my own family was here at last and I couldn't have been happier. And next year, I thought to myself, I will be creating this magic with my Skyla included. Life really couldn't get any better.

Christmas morning arrived and I was so happy to be woken by an excited Tiffany shouting "Daddy, Daddy, it's Christmas".

"Merry Christmas Tiffany" I shouted and got out of bed and pulled on my dressing gown.

"Come on Tiffany" I called, "Let's see if Father Christmas has been". We ran down the stairs and I watched with a real feeling of contentment as I watched the girls tear the paper from their gifts. They couldn't wait to get out into the garden with their car so I put the turkey that I had already prepared the night before in the oven, wrapped them up in warm clothes and spent an hour outside with them running up and down the garden path with the pair of them in the car.

Right, time to get organised. I had planned a full-on Christmas Dinner and there were things that needed to be done. "Can I do anything?" Ann asked.

"Nope" I said proudly. "It's under control, you just sit back and watch the kids".

She smiled happily and left me to it.

Everything was cooking away nicely, and I was just putting the finishing touches to the dinner table. Place mats, napkins, cutlery laid out correctly. A highchair was in the place of one dining room chair for Tammie to join us for some dinner. I was so excited. This was everything I had imagined. A perfect family Christmas. Everything was ready to be served up when then there was a knock at the door. I peered round the kitchen door and looked at Ann with a puzzled expression.

"I'll get it" she said heaving herself off the sofa.

"OK, but I'm serving up" I shouted. Then I heard shouts of "Nanny, Nanny" from Tiffany. "What the fuck" I muttered under my breath. I wiped my hands on a nearby tea-towel and popped my head round the doorway.

"Merry Christmas" she said cheerily, starting to take off her coat.

"Erm Lynne, you're not supposed to be here until about 4" I muttered nervously.

"Oh, well, I couldn't wait to see my grandchildren and watch them open their presents" she replied, still with a big grin on her face and lifting Tammie into her arms.

I was beginning to feel both uncomfortable and a bit cross. "Well, we're just about to eat" I pointed out.

"Oh, well don't mind me." I couldn't believe my ears.

"Lynne, I pressed, "we are about to sit down to eat as a family, we agreed yesterday that you would be here later. I'm sure you understand. And if you come back later, we can all have a good time together with the girls watching them enjoy their presents".

She glared at me, and I could see the anger starting to bubble. "Well, I'm going to see my dad later now and I want to see MY grandchildren now".

I matched her tone with a stern. "I'm sorry Lynne, we are about to eat, you will have to come back later".

Lynne turned and looked at Ann. "Are you hearing this Ann? He's trying to kick me out of YOUR house" she said.

Ann lowered her head and muttered something that I couldn't hear.

"It's OUR house" I shot back "and I really don't want to fall out, but our dinner is getting cold". I looked at her with what I hoped was a stern but pleading look. "Please Lynne, can we just stick to the original plan, and we will see you later?"

"Forget it!" she snapped. "Have Christmas to yourself you selfish bastard. Thanks for ruining mine, I only wanted to see my grandchildren" She put Tammie down.

"Your presents are there girls" she said pointing at the bag of gifts that she had dropped next to the sofa she had been about to make herself comfortable on, pulled her coat back over her shoulders and stormed out.

The door slammed behind her and both I and Ann winced.

I looked at Ann unsure what her reaction was going to be. After all, it was her Mum and I hadn't wanted to cause an argument between them, but I didn't want all my hard work to have been ruined either! Ann looked back at me and just shrugged her shoulders. "Don't worry about it" she said. "She gets like that; she doesn't like it much that you are looking after me and I am not relying on her as much" she explained. "She's been dropping hints loads lately about me not asking her for help as much and I think she is just feeling a bit pushed out".

I put my arm around her and promised that I would try to make it up to her Mum later. It wasn't the start to my first family Christmas dinner that I had planned, but we quickly moved on and settled down to enjoy the rest of the day. I had expected Lynne to come back at around 4, but sadly, it seemed that she was too upset to bury the hatchet and she didn't make another appearance that day.

The Christmas period passed with the usual visits to various family members, but Lynne continued to stay away with the only contact being a couple of angry text messages to Ann demanding that I apologise for "kicking her out". I didn't see that I had done anything wrong and am incredibly stubborn but agreed that I would "let it go" and just continue our relationship as though nothing had happened next time Lynne came round, or we went to visit. Ann knew her mum best and she told me that the best thing to do was to just let her cool down and in a few days Lynne was bound to make contact wanting to see the kids again and we should all just act as though nothing had happened. It seemed the best way forward to me.

I really didn't want to continue any bad feeling. Ann was due to give birth to Lynne's third grandchild in just a few weeks and it made sense that we all pull together as a family to make sure that the occasion was as happy as it should be.

I was working New Year's Eve but due to finish at about 9. I couldn't wait. 2019 was primed and ready to be the best! I had some beers chilling in the fridge and although Ann couldn't drink, I had bought her a bottle of alcohol-free bubbly for the occasion.

I got home from work, and we spent a quiet night in front of the TV and chatting about the year ahead and all the excitement that was to come. "Happy New Year!!" We clinked glasses as 2018 came to a close and 2019 was brought in to the sounds of Auld Lang Syne on the TV and I daydreamed about my life to come. My life as stepfather to two beautiful little girls, a new daddy to my own baby was so nearly here. An uncle to my brother's little girl (Ash and Jade had discovered they were also having a little girl). I smiled to myself as I imagined the close bond these two little girls were bound to develop growing up so close in age with each other. They were going to be so spoilt. After the initial shock and backlash at the announcement of Jade's pregnancy, things had calmed down and my mum was visibly beside herself with excitement at the thought of these two new babies coming into the family. Even my dad was excited, although he probably would never have admitted it.

"2019, here I come" I thought happily. Little did I know that the disagreement with Lynne on Christmas Day was going to have a ripple effect for the next two years to come. I believe it was THAT disagreement that set Lynne on a path to ensure I was not a part of her family at any cost.

New Year's Day started in the usual way. Tammie and Tiffany playing with their toys while I prepared their breakfast and Ann sat on the sofa scrolling through her phone. "What!" She suddenly shouted.

I looked up in surprise "What's up?"

"You aren't going to fucking believe this" she said.

I walked over to where she was sat and took a seat next to her. She handed me her phone which was open at her Facebook messages.

There was a message from Lynne.

(Lynne) *Why are you letting Carl hurt Tammie?*

"Eh?" I didn't understand. She took the phone from me and tapped out a message.

(Ann) *What?*
(Lynne) *I've seen the picture*
(Ann) *What?*
(Lynne) *Carl is hurting Tammie. You put it on Facebook.*
(Ann) *What are you talking about?*

I was racking my brains trying to think what she could possibly mean. I started scrolling through my Facebook feed to see if I could see what the hell she could possibly be talking about, but there was nothing.

Then Lynne sent a picture to Ann. It was a photograph of Tammie and Tiffany on the sofa in matching Peppa Pig pyjamas. Ann had wanted the picture to send to my aunt who had bought them as a gift for the girls for Christmas. Tiffany was smiling happily in the photo, but Tammie was clearly unhappy about having her photo taken and was throwing a little strop. We had sat them on the sofa, but Tammie was perilously close to the edge and as Ann snapped the photo on her phone you could see my arm in the shot holding Tammie's leg to keep her from falling off the edge.

Lynne was claiming that the reason that Tammie looked unhappy in the photograph was because I was pinching her leg.

Ann quickly typed a response telling her mum how ridiculous she was being but was visibly shaken when she received the next response.

(Lynne) *I have reported you both to Social Services and I am applying for custody.*

Ann gasped. What the fuck? "I can't believe she would do this" Ann said starting to cry.

I was gobsmacked. I would never hurt a child and particularly not these two little girls that I adored.

"Don't worry" I said reassuringly to Ann, we haven't done anything wrong, and nobody is taking your children away from you.

Of course, I was worried. I didn't have any experience of dealing with things like this, but I was sure that children wouldn't be removed from their mother over an innocent photograph. Then a sudden horrific thought entered my head. What if they said I couldn't be around the girls anymore? What if they said I couldn't live with my new baby? I tapped out an angry message to Lynne letting her know that I would never hurt a child and that I couldn't believe that she would report her own daughter to Social Services. I did not receive a reply.

"I can't believe this" I said to Ann. "I haven't done anything wrong".

"I know".

"That's it". Ann said firmly, "she is never going to see me or the kids again".

I won't deny that I felt a sense of relief that Ann was backing me, but I was sad that a minor disagreement over a Christmas visit had ended like this. I was also worried about the possible involvement of Social Services.

Later that day myself and Ann took the kids to see my nan. She used to work for a legal firm and always had a common-sense approach to most problems and I valued her opinion. We told her what had happened and showed her the texts and the 'incriminating' photo.

"Can she really apply for custody?" Ann asked my nan.

Nan shook her head.

"Well, she CAN", she said, "but the chance of her getting it is near impossible and it would cost her a lot of money to have that heard in the Family Court".

I felt a huge sense of relief and I could see that Ann felt better just hearing it from someone else.

Later that week we received a visit from Social Services. We sat down and spoke with her and I knew she was watching intently as I interacted with Tiffany and Tammie, but we were so relieved when she told us pretty much right at the beginning that they knew that this was a 'malicious' report but that they were duty bound to investigate any allegations like this that were made.

She left and after a few days we received an email confirming that Social Services were closing the case. Phew, what a relief. But I couldn't get my head round how a mother could do that to her own daughter. It was beyond belief.

I was glad that nothing had come of it. I had known deep down that it would be OK because I had done nothing wrong, but still, there is always that element of doubt. Unfortunately, Lynne was not so happy with the outcome and the abusive messages from Ann's brother soon started.

He seemed to be angry at the supposed abuse I was inflicting on his niece. I admit to being a little worried as his reputation for violence and drug use was well known. I wasn't worried about my own safety as I could look after myself, but I was certainly worried about Ann. I installed some security cameras around the perimeter of the house just to be sure and ignored the threats that were received frequently.

By mid-January, Ann was suffering terribly with hip dysplasia due to the pregnancy. She was in constant agony, and I lost count of the calls made to the medical team. At one point, Ann begged them to induce labour to make the pain stop. I was becoming more and more frustrated. It was horrendous watching the woman I loved in so much pain and I just felt that the medical team weren't taking her pain seriously. But we soldiered on. I was having to take more and more time off work as Ann would become so upset as I tried to get ready for my shift and crying that she couldn't possibly look after Tiffany and Tammie when she couldn't even stand up. My impeccable attendance record at work was now marred with scores of absences and I knew they were getting a little fed up with it.

I didn't want to mention it to Ann, she was really struggling. She didn't have her Mum to lean on anymore. My own mum and my dad had been an absolute God send picking up the slack and helping wherever they could. My mum was always looking after the girls when Ann was too tired or in too much pain and I had to work, but still things were becoming difficult. I also didn't want to mention work not being as supportive as Ann thought they should be. I did find her attitude to employment quite amusing. She seemed to have this idea that I was doing them a favour by working for them, rather than me having an obligation to meet my contracted hours in return for a half decent wage.

On more than one occasion Ann told me that I had to ask them to reduce my hours once the baby was born.

"I can't do that", I said "We are going to need all the money we can get".

"Well we can make up the difference in benefits" she replied. "At the very least you have to tell your work that you have to have regular hours from now on. You have a family now and they will have to understand that".

Of course, I knew it didn't work that way, but I didn't want to argue so I just reassured her that we would cope.

Family Man

February arrived and I waited excitedly for the birth of my baby girl. Early on the 12th February 2019, Ann told me that she needed to go to the hospital

"Are you in labour?" I asked excitedly.

"No". She said shaking her head and looking worried.

"What's up?" the panic evident in my voice.

"I haven't felt her move for ages".

"What? When?" I felt sick.

"Since yesterday".

I outwardly tried to stay calm, but inside I was in a hell of a state.

"Don't worry" I said trying to sound calmer than I felt, "I'll ring Mum and see if she can look after the girls and we will get to the hospital".

She nodded in agreement.

"I'm sure it will be fine,"

I rang Mum and within the hour both she and Dad had arrived at our house. Mum came to look after the girls while Dad drove us up to the hospital on his way to work. We waited for what seemed an age to be seen by a Doctor who was concerned enough to organise an ambulance to transfer us to Gloucester Hospital.

There were lots of "It's just a precaution's", "No need to worry", etc., but I was freaking out. I was allowed to ride with Ann in the ambulance and I spent the time just trying to stay calm enough so that I could look calm to her, but inside I was terrified that something was terribly wrong.

I don't remember too much of what happened after that, only that we were relieved to be told that Skyla was fine, and more than ready to make her entrance into the world and they decided the best thing to do would be to induce labour. I was so happy. Not only was my baby OK after the worry of this morning, but I was going to meet her. Soon!

I won't bore you with the details of the labour as it was pretty uneventful and I imagine that if Skyla is reading this now, she probably doesn't want to know the gory details, so I will just cut straight to the moment she was placed in my arms.

I feel like there should be a big blank white space here now. We already know I am no good with words for everyday events but this! Wow! In that moment there were far too many emotions to count. Love, happiness, fear, trepidation, awe, pride and oh so many more. My life had changed in this single moment. I had always known I wanted to be a dad. I thought I was a pretty good dad to my two stepchildren, but suddenly, this tiny being in my arms meant that I was no longer sure I was up to the job. This little girl was everything and it was up to me to make sure she had everything she needed in this world to thrive. My world was complete. Skyla Harris Organ had arrived.

Just 10 days after Skyla's arrival, Mia Grace, Ashley and Jade's baby arrived. I was over the moon. It was so exciting to know that these two little girls were going to grow up together. My whole family were on cloud nine for days. Facebook was bombarded with different photo albums. There were pictures of Skyla, pictures of Skyla with Tammie and Tiffany, pictures of Mia, pictures of Skyla and Mia, pictures of Mia with Tiffany and Tammie and of course pictures of everybody you could fit into one frame. I imagine that the whole family's Facebook friends list would be completely informed and maybe a little bored of the two new arrivals to the Organ family.

The only fly in the ointment was the lack of contact from Lynne. Ann had sent her a picture a few hours after she was born and the only response she got was "told you she would be born close to Nan's Birthday." I thought it was an odd response, but nothing was going to spoil my happiness at this point, although I did feel a bit sad for Ann and the girls.

Tiffany and Tammie were very excited about their new little sister. Tammie still hadn't shown any signs of talking but her delight at watching Skyla was evident and it was quite difficult to dissuade Tiffany from helping with every feed and nappy change.

I threw myself into being the best father I possibly could be. Despite working full time and odd hours I was determined to be a hands-on dad. Ann told me she was finding it difficult to cope while I was work and would constantly ask me if I had managed to drop my hours yet. I knew that this wasn't going to be possible, so I just made excuses and concentrated on making sure that when I WAS at home Ann had all the support that she needed and would make sure that I was the first one out of bed when Skyla cried in the night or if one of the girls came into the bedroom for whatever reason.

One day in April I came home from work and Ann seemed to have cheered up.

"You look happy" I said, pleased to see her smile for the first time in ages.

"I've got a job interview" she said.

I was a bit surprised. I hadn't even known that she had been thinking of getting a job. It seemed a little odd, Skyla was barely 8 weeks old and of course there was Tiffany and Tammie to consider too.

"Yeah," she said, "I was thinking, I really want to earn some money so we can afford nice things for the girls, and also, I don't want Skyla to be as clingy with me as Tammie is, so I thought I would get some part time work".

"How is that going to work though?" I said.

She glared at me

"Well, if you drop your hours, we can make sure that one of us is always home" she snapped as though I was stupid.

I didn't want to dampen her new enthusiasm so I had a chat with Mum, and we felt that between us we could make sure that there was childcare to cover any hours that Ann got. Ann was happy with this, however, when she was offered the job it was clear that it just wouldn't work. The hours that she would have to work were too erratic and we couldn't possibly guarantee that we would always have childcare.

Ann was beside herself and it broke my heart to see her so miserable as she tried to think of ways to make it work.

"Please" she begged me, "Can't you go part time?"

"What's the point of that?" I asked, you wouldn't earn as much as me, so we would be worse off".

"I don't care about the money; I just want to go to work. I can't cope with the three kids all the time; I need some time to myself. I need a life" she stated.

I could see her point of view, so I tentatively broached the subject with my manager. It turned out that it might be possible, but I would have to make a 'flexible working request', which sounded promising. The only problem was that it could take up to 12 weeks for everything to go through, and it might not be approved.

"Please Carl" Ann begged.
"We can cope on my wage and benefits and I have the child maintenance from Mike" she reasoned.
And in a moment of madness I agreed. I quit my job. I would have done anything to make Ann happy and there was a part of me that was excited about being a 'Stay at home' Dad, but I couldn't shift that nagging feeling in the pit of my stomach that this was a really bad decision.

One week later, Ann seemed on top of the world as she had completed her induction week. I was settling into my new role as 'home maker' and chuffed that Ann was settling into working life so well. Everything was going to be fine. And it was! For two whole weeks. Ann came home from work after her shift during week three and told me she had quit.

"What?" I cried. "What do you mean, you've quit?".
"I can't do it" she said, "the cleaning stuff that they make me do is making my eczema play up and it's really painful" she whined.
I couldn't believe it. Of all the stupid decisions to make without even raising it with me. A fleeting thought entered my head that this had all been somehow contrived to ensure I was at home more often, and that I had been expertly manipulated in some way, but I pushed it to the back of my mind. But still, now what were we going to do?

Things became quite strained between us over the next few weeks as the routine I had established in the short time that Ann had dabbled in working life continued and Ann pretty much spent the day scrolling through her mobile phone or watching TV. One evening, after I had settled the kids into bed and was preparing the bottles ready for the night feeds, Ann casually said

"Oh, I'm taking the kids to see my mum tomorrow".

I was a bit shocked.

"Oh, erm how did that come about?" I asked.

"Oh, we've been messaging each other for a while".

"You never said?"

"Well, she doesn't want to see you" she said sheepishly.

"Fine by me" I shrugged.

"Will you be OK with Skyla on your own for the night?" she asked, "I want to stay over with Tammie and Tiffany because they've missed her."

I looked up sharply,

"What about Skyla?" I asked. Ann looked embarrassed.

"She says there isn't really room for the baby to stay the night as well" she said quietly.

"Oh right". I was astounded. She hadn't even met her newest granddaughter yet and it was evident that she was in no rush to do so.

I can't say that I wasn't pleased that Skyla wouldn't be taken into a home full of smokers. I lost count of the times I had to strip Tiffany and Tammie off after they had returned from a night at Nanny's because they stank of cigarette smoke, but it had never been anything I had felt I could comment on. However, when it came to my own daughter it was an entirely different matter, so I was glad that it wasn't a conversation I had to have just yet. But really? Was she really not going to acknowledge Skyla's existence at all because she no longer approved of me? It certainly seemed that way.

And that is how a pattern slowly started to form. Ann would often visit her mum with Tammie and Tiffany and I would visit my own parents with Skyla. Where my mum and dad had previously been heralded by Ann as her absolute 'Rock' and she had liked nothing more than spending time with my family, all of a sudden, she didn't want to visit them with me anymore and made excuses not to come with me to evenings out. I suppose I was relieved that while Ann seemed to be drifting away from my mum and dad in favour of spending time with her own mum, I at least didn't have to fight to have Skyla spend time with them.

Lynne would often pop by to drop Tammie and Tiffany home or collect them for another overnight stay and each time she completely blanked me. At the same time, Ann's behaviour was becoming more and more difficult to handle. I just couldn't do anything right and it seemed that she would do anything to stop me spending time away from her. I cancelled my gym membership as I just didn't have the time to visit. Ann would often moan that she wanted to do more things as a family and so I would arrange things that we could afford. A day out at the park for all of us, Skyla's first swimming trip, but each time I was ready to go, Ann would make excuses not to come. Even worse, she would convince me not to do them either. My life had become a constant cycle of seeing to the children in between scrolling mindlessly through social media whilst staring at a TV screen. My only respite was when Ann was with her mum, and I could take Skyla out on my own.

Evenings out either with or without Ann rarely happened anymore and people were starting to notice.
"Everything OK?" Mum or Dad would ask.
"Fine" was my stock answer.
It seemed that Ann was beginning to go to some extreme lengths to stop me from going out or spending time with anyone else. My brothers 21st birthday was a prime example. A family meal had been arranged and of course my new family were invited. Ann surprised me by agreeing to come and I was so excited. Only about an hour before we were due to be at the venue, Ann suddenly announced that Tammie was unwell and needed to go to the hospital.
"What?" I asked, "what's wrong with her?". Of course, Tammie still wasn't talking but I hadn't noticed anything out of the norm, and I had spent the entire day with her.
"She has a fever" she said crossly.
"No, she doesn't".

"I know my own daughter" she spat whilst dialling her mother's number.

Within 10 minutes Lynne was at the door and they were bundling Tiffany and Tammie into her car and driving off up the road. I couldn't believe my eyes. There was nothing wrong with Tammie and I was sure that it was all an excuse not to come out with me. It was ridiculous. I wasn't forcing her to come but I couldn't for the life of me understand why she didn't want to have a nice evening out.

I couldn't let my brother down on his 21st birthday and there seemed little point staying in on my own for the sake of it, so I continued with my plans to celebrate Ash's birthday with Skyla.

That night I was bombarded with message after message telling me that I was the worst father in the world for not caring about Tammie. Literally dozens of abusive messages. She claimed that she was at Gloucester hospital with Tammie, but I had my doubts. When Tammie was "discharged" a couple of hours later I received the message
"Staying at Mum's, have fun with your wonderful family."

Things went from bad to worse. After the 21st Birthday episode, Ann seemed to take an absurd dislike for my family. My mum had uploaded some photos to Facebook that included Tiffany and Tammie as she had done a hundred times before, but this time Ann was furious,
"How dare she" she yelled. "She didn't ask me if she could".
I just stared at her not knowing what to say. This was getting ridiculous and I felt torn. I wanted to defend and back my girlfriend, but I felt like I was being asked to attack my mum for something that was so trivial and harmless.

I begged her not to, but Ann composed and sent a blunt message to my Mum "ASK before you post pictures of MY daughters on Facebook!" My Mum was clearly shocked and hurt as I received a questioning message. She was mortified. She certainly hadn't wanted to upset Ann, but she was also obviously confused as to where this had come from? She had never been asked not to post pictures of Tiffany and Tammie before. They WERE part of our family.

Slowly and systematically, without me even knowing when it started or the speed it happened, I was spending less and less time outside of our home. Every waking moment was now with Ann and the kids. To do anything else was more trouble than it was worth. Mum, Dad, Ash and Nan constantly invited me to family outings and every time I was excited to accept and tell them that we would ALL be there, only for Ann to make excuses just moments before we were due to leave for anywhere.

Ann started to openly criticise my family to me.

"They control you" she would state. "They are trying to boss you around again".

"They just invited us out for a meal and offered to pay" I would reply. "That's a nice thing to do, they just want to spend time with us".

"Control!" She would say firmly.

I never believed what she was saying. I knew it wasn't control. I was proud that I was part of such a close and supportive family, and it was that exact kind of family I was trying to build for myself with Ann and the girls. I was starting to slide down a slippery slope into blackness. I loved Ann. Wanted to marry her but everything I said or did seemed to piss her off. I made a conscious effort to try harder. I stopped returning everyone's calls and decided to make myself happy with just this small family. It broke my heart, but I wanted this to work so much.

I was falling deeper and deeper into a depression. I looked around me and all I could see was blackness. The only light was Skyla. Apart from her I felt completely alone. I so wanted to reach out but to do so would mean answering questions that I just didn't want to. Because answering questions would mean that I had to look at my relationship more closely and admit that things were not right.

One Saturday morning in October, Ann, Tiffany, and Tammie had been collected to spend the day with Lynne again and I was left to do the shopping with Skyla. I strapped Skyla into her pushchair and started the walk into town when I heard my name being called.

"Carl" shouted my nan. I half turned around. A fleeting idea to pretend I hadn't heard her and keep on walking entered my head. I didn't want this conversation. It was too hard. I knew what was coming. All the questions, demands that I answer them. Demand to know why I hadn't visited her for months. Demands that I choose.

I didn't want to choose. I wanted Ann. I wanted my family. I didn't want to bloody choose, but if forced to I knew what I would do. Skyla. I choose Skyla. I would ALWAYS choose Skyla.

I stopped and turned to look at my nan. She looked out of breath and slightly frantic as she rushed to try to catch me up. I had to stop and wait, before she hurt herself. She reached me and looked at me with a pleading look in her eyes.
"Can we go for a coffee?" She asked. I nodded.
"Come on." She said taking my arm.

We found a small table at a coffee shop in Cirencester and I settled Skyla down while Nan got the coffee. I sat and waited wondering what I was going to say. Preparing to defend my family and justify everything that I knew my family disapproved of.

Nan sat down.
"What's going on Carl?"
I looked at her.
"Why won't you talk to me anymore?"
In that moment I felt more wretched than I had ever felt. My nan who had always been my confidant and on my side, looked heartbroken.

"Nothing". I muttered. "I just can't do anything right". And suddenly, all my feelings bubbled to the surface and I could feel tears pricking my eyes. And it all came out. How just to keep the peace I stayed at home doing absolutely nothing all day.
A few moments later my aunt joined us. She had driven my nan to come and find me that morning as Nan had been so upset about the situation.

My Aunt Rachel takes after my nan and doesn't mince her words either and got straight to the point.
"We all know what's going on Carl."
I looked at her blankly.

"You don't have to choose" she said forcibly. "Ann can try to alienate you from us as much as she likes, but we are going nowhere. You don't have to choose because we will always be here".

"And if Ann is what you want and she comes as part of the package, then we accept her too. We don't have to like her or what she is doing. We just love YOU and want you to be happy".

I didn't know what to say. I felt like an enormous weight had been lifted and a sense of shame for not trusting that the people I love would understand.

"Visit with Ann, visit without Ann." She continued. "We don't care, we just care that you visit sometimes. Or send a message, pick up the phone. Something, anything, just don't shut us out. You are breaking your mum's heart."

"And mine" said Nan miserably.

I felt ashamed but I was also relieved. They got it. They understood. The penny kind of dropped for me then too. There was no problem here. I COULD have it all. If Ann didn't want to come with me when I spent time with my friends or family, that was fine, but it didn't mean I had to stop completely. I think that was the turning point for me, but it was most definitely the turning point for Ann, I just didn't know it.

It wasn't an 'Announcement' to Ann, rather a change of behaviour. I no longer mentioned things that I wanted to do, judged her reaction, and then acted in a way that would make her happy. I now just told her honestly what I was going to do and told her she was welcome to join me.

The first couple of times worked well. I was surprised but happy. Why hadn't I done this before rather than pussyfooting around, I thought to myself, but again very quickly Ann started to show how unhappy she was with my arrangements. This time she started picking arguments shortly before I was due to leave. I stood my ground. The next step was tears and the accusation that I didn't want to spend any time with her.

"I want nothing more" I argued. "Please, come with me."

But she always refused.

Early November, I planned to spend the day at my mum and dad's house with my dad and brother watching rugby and then football. It was all planned, and as was usual Ann started to make waves. She stayed the night at her mum's with Tiffany and Tammie, leaving me again with Skyla. I am not sure if she thought this would mean I wouldn't go to my dad's as drinking had been involved in the original plans, but it was easy just to take Skyla and not drink.

I got up on the Saturday morning and got Skyla ready, along with the usual paraphernalia that come with spending time away from the home with a small baby. Dad offered to pick me up at the same time as he picked Ashley up (Ashley and Jade had moved into their own flat back in April) and so I put Skyla into the travel chair so that it could be strapped safely into the car.

The afternoon passed pleasantly until the text messages from Ann started.

(Ann) *When are you coming home?*
    (Me) *Later. Watching football*
(Ann) *I've cooked tea*
    (Me) *Why? I told you I would be late.*
(Ann) *I want to see my baby.*
    (Me) *Come round here then. Jade and Ash are here.*
(Ann) *No. Come home.*

At that point I started to ignore the messages, but they just kept on coming. I turned my phone to silent, but could still hear and feel the vibrations signalling that yet another message has been received.

I kept glancing at the front screen to read the messages turning from declarations of love, to threats that if I didn't return home immediately I shouldn't return at all.

I really didn't want to go home for another row, and I knew that was exactly what I would get if I went home now so I took a deep breath and tapped out a message.

    (Me) *Skyla is settled. I'm going to stay here tonight and I will see you in the morning.*

There was no response and I felt relieved as I settled down to enjoy the footie. My mum was there and offered me a beer assuring me that she could take care of Skyla if needed.

Mum settled Skyla into my old bedroom and after Ash had left to go home, I made my way up the stairs.

I climbed into bed and stared at the ceiling. "I'm in for it tomorrow" I thought. But I really couldn't face going home and listening to the same old complaints from Ann about me not spending time with her. I really was beginning to get fed up with never being able to spend time outside of the house, but Ann spent so much time with Lynne and of course I was never invited. I had been feeling lonely and re-establishing my relationships with my family had been the tonic that I hadn't known I had needed.

"Oh well" I thought to myself. "I'll face the music tomorrow" and settled down to sleep. At around 1:00am I was woken by Mum calling for me from my doorway.

"What is it?" I said, instinctively looking for Skyla in her carrier. I could see she was fast asleep so looked at Mum questioningly.

"Come downstairs" she whispered.

I felt confused but crawled quietly out of bed. I pulled on my trousers and made my way downstairs to be greeted by two police officers in the living room.

"Mr Organ?" said the male officer
"Yeah"
"We've had a complaint that we need to investigate" he explained. I looked at him blankly. I had no idea what he was talking about.
"Is Skyla here?" He enquired.
"Yeah, she's asleep upstairs" I replied defensively.
What was all this about? Was I being accused of kidnap or something?
"Mr Organ, we've received a report from Miss Green that you smacked Skyla." "What?" I almost shouted.

The police officer put out his hand as a sign that I should remain calm.

"She says that her daughter told her that she saw you smack her on the leg this morning when you were changing her nappy". I couldn't believe my ears.

"What? Why?" I said.

"I have to ask, Mr Organ. Have you smacked your baby?"

"NO" I said emphatically.

He nodded. "OK, well, just to put everyone's mind at rest, would it be possible for us to see Skyla?"

"She's sleeping".

He looked at me kindly.

"I know, but it really would just put the matter to rest, and you can go back to sleep and we can reassure Miss Green that Skyla is safe".

"Well of course she's safe, she's with her dad" I said.

We stared at each other and he just said

"Please, it really would be best all round if we could just take a look at the baby".

I nodded and signalled for them to follow me to my old bedroom where Skyla was sleeping. Both police officers entered the dark room. I pointed to where Skyla was sleeping.

"See, she's fine" I said.

"Mr Organ" said the officer. "I'm really sorry, but we are going to need you to undress her so we can see her bottom and legs".

"What??" I said angrily. "She's bloody sleeping and there's nothing wrong with her legs".

My mum rushed in.

"Carl, just undress her and show them and then they can see this is just stupid", she said calmly.

I was furious.

"They are just doing their job Carl" Mum said.

I took a deep breath and nodded. I carefully picked up Skyla from her baby seat and placed her on my bed. She stirred but didn't wake. I undid her baby-grow and stripped her down to her nappy. The female officer stepped forward and smiled at me kindly. The room was only lit by the landing light so that we disturbed Skyla as little as possible. The officer took out her torch and I put my hand over Skyla's eyes to protect her from as much glare as I could. She shone the torch over

Skyla's legs and I gently lifted them up so that she could see the back of them too.

"Do you want me to take her nappy off?" I asked in a curt tone.

"No", she responded, "I think we've disturbed you enough for tonight". She switched off the torch. "We'll leave you to settle her down again and see you downstairs?" She asked. I nodded.

Carefully I re-dressed my little girl and put her back to bed. Thankfully, she hadn't been woken fully and quickly drifted back to sleep without too much trouble.

I made my way downstairs where I was greeted by Mum, Dad, and the police officers.

"We had to investigate." I heard the man say.

"Yeah, I understand" said my dad, "but you can see its rubbish?"

The PC nodded. "Mr Organ", he said turning to me "Again, we are really sorry for disturbing you and your family so late at night, but I am sure you understand that we had to investigate such a serious claim as quickly as possible."

I nodded.

"We'll let the complainant know that the baby is safe".

They left the house leaving me with a fury bubbling up inside. Fury and devastation. What the fuck was going on now? How could she do such a thing. I knew damn well that Tiffany had said no such thing of her own free will. Tiffany was quite a precocious 4-year-old by this time and easily bribed with a glittery toy or a bag of sweeties. If she had even said it at all. At no time did the police tell me that they had heard it from Tiffany.

Much later in the lengthy proceedings that were to follow, I obtained a copy of the police Records pertaining to the case.

It clearly stated that the initial call to the police had been made by Ann Green on 2nd November at 16:21. I checked my phone and saw that this was just moments after I sent the message that I would be staying the night at my parents. What the hell was she thinking? Did she think that they would come and take Skyla from me as some kind of punishment? To force me to go home? Or to keep me away? I couldn't make any sense of it.

Although I was unaware of it at the time, the police report showed that Ann had already ended our relationship and begun to spin a web of lies that would almost choke me in months to come.

The report said the following:

The caller (Ann) had an 8-month-old child with ex-partner.
He has collected child from address today.
Prior to leaving callers 4-year-old child has witnessed the male hit the child.
Male has left the address with the child and refuses to bring the child back
Father is paternal Father and no order in place stopping him having access to children.

Physical harm – Male has been witnessed to hit the child. Caller is not aware of any physical injuries
Emotional – Caller is very distressed by incident today.
Caller is awaiting mediation currently regarding child custody.

As I read on, it was clear by the next section of the report that the police had suspicions that this was not a genuine call. The call was reviewed at 23:50 according to the log.

Caller states she was aware of the alleged assault on her baby prior to allowing the child to go with her father. If this is the case, why has she allowed the child to go?

What is meant by not aware of any physical injuries? Either there are visible injuries or there are not?

What actions has the caller taken to go to the address she knows/believes the child to be at?

Why does the caller believe that the child's Father will not be able to obtain more formula for his child?

Caller needs to be spoken to again in the first instance despite the time of night as this incident has not been properly reviewed earlier.

At this point it is clear that the police attempted to contact Ann by telephone at 00:13am. It is now the 3rd November.

No reply from caller. Will attend the address to speak to her first

00:21 – No reply at the door. Will attend Fathers address

The log is later updated at 01:38

I have attended and spoken to the caller, she has stated her other Daughter mentioned the incident after her partner had left, so she didn't have a chance to check Skyla. She didn't think that Carl would have any formula as he didn't take any and doesn't have much money. She didn't want to go and speak to him at the address as she didn't want to cause any further problems as she has a difficult relationship with Carl's family.

I have then attended Carl's parents address who were shocked to see me. Skyla was comfortably asleep in her cot in a baby grow. Carl removed the lower half of the baby grow so I could check Skyla's legs, but Skyla then started to stir, and I do not propose waking Skyla up at 00:00 when she is contently sleeping. I could not see any injuries or marks on Skyla and have no concerns regarding Skyla staying with Carl and his parents. The house is very well kept and the family although shocked were happy to assist me.

No longer feeling tired I sat in the living room mulling things over. One thing was clear. My relationship was over. My dream of a happy family shattered. And why?

I nodded off on the sofa and was woken the next morning by Skyla crying. I felt miserable but life had to go on for her. Mum was already up and seeing to her when I made my way upstairs.

"You OK?" she asked looking at me sadly.

"Not really."

"That's the last nappy" she said, pointing at the fresh nappy on Skyla's bum.

I sighed. What was I supposed to do now? I couldn't go 'home'. I was now officially homeless I suppose. I made a quick call to my nan who arrived within 20 minutes. She reacted the way Nan always reacts. A mixture of anger for what Ann had done and heartbreak for me and wanting to make it all better.

"Can we go and get Skyla some stuff?" I asked her.
"Of course," she replied straight away.
I left Skyla with Mum and Dad and jumped in the car with Nan.
"What are you going to do?" She asked softly.
"I don't know, what CAN I do? I have to go home; I've got nowhere to live."
"Don't be daft, your dad will have you back in a shot – he won't want you going back to Ann after what she has done. How can you ever trust her?"
"I know, but what about Skyla?"
"Look Carl" Nan said, "Do you really think that if you go back with Skyla now that things can go back to the way they were?"
I shook my head
"No, she will take Skyla, kick you out and there is no way she is going to let you see Skyla again. She has already started lying to try to have her taken from you".
I nodded again, realisation feeling like it was about to drown me.
"Well, she won't stop you seeing my great grandchild" she said firmly. "Over my dead body".

We did a small shop at Tesco, picking up a couple of new outfits for Skyla, more formula (although please be assured, reader, I had more than enough for at least 3 more feeds) and of course nappies.

Somewhere along the line my aunt Rachel had been told the story and she was already at the house when we returned. Rachel with her calm head was ready to talk about the next step. It had already been decided that I was moving back into my old room with Skyla. It was a Sunday so not much could be done to start the Family Court process, but we all agreed that the only way to ensure that I had regular access to Skyla was to have a firm order from the courts. In the meantime, I intended for Skyla to stay with me so that Ann wouldn't have the opportunity to make up any more lies.

It was around 10:30am by this time and Ann had sent just one text message. I almost laughed out loud as I read her message asking when I was coming home.

After last night? Did she imagine that I was just going to stroll through the door like nothing had happened? She had accused me of child abuse for heaven's sake.

At around 11:00am there was a knock at the door.
"I'll get it" said Rachel.
I felt nervous. I heard talking and then Rachel called me over.
"She says she just wants to talk to you".
I walked past my mum who was changing Skyla's nappy on the changing mat on the floor and closed the kitchen door behind me.

I looked at Ann angrily.
"When are you coming home?" She demanded.
"Err, never" I replied matching her angry tone.
With that she pushed past me to the door and marched into the living room. I watched with amazement as she strode straight to my mum and without saying a single word put her arms out as if to say 'Give her to me' but no words were spoken.

"She's being changed!" Said Rachel sternly.
Incredibly Ann literally stamped her foot to the floor, turned and marched straight back out again. It was very strange, and I couldn't help but feel a little shell-shocked by the whole thing.

"Right" said Rachel, "Let's get things sorted, you need to get your stuff out of Ann's house".
"How are we going to do that?" I asked.
Rachel was already on her phone and I heard her say
"Hi, I wondered if you could help, we were wondering if there was a possibility of having a police presence for a retrieval of property in order to prevent a breach of the peace".
I smiled. Rachel always knew how to handle stuff like this.

I heard her go into detail about the history and explain to the call handler that while there was no intention for me to breach the peace, she was fairly sure that things weren't going to go as quietly as we would certainly hope. The call ended with disappointment and Rachel curtly ended with, "Well, I realise that, but please log this call as I am more than certain that Miss Green will be making a call to you making a nonsense complaint".

Rachel hung up and said
"Come on Carl, we will have to do it without them".
I jumped into Rachel's car and Dad followed on behind in his to ensure that we had enough room to transport all my possessions. Skyla stayed behind with Mum. On the way there, Rachel gave me instructions. "Stay calm". "Don't raise your voice". "Be quick, take only what is yours and Skyla's and get out as quickly as possible". "Don't even talk to her".

My heart was pounding as we made our way to the front door. Rachel got her phone out and started video recording. I looked at her questioningly.
"I'm not stupid" she said smiling "We know how she likes to make stuff up, so we had best record it to show exactly what happens".
I took my keys out and tried to unlock the door. But the key wouldn't fit? What? When had she changed the bloody locks? It was 12 o'clock on a Sunday! I rang the doorbell and Ann half opened it and shoved a large Tesco 'Bag for Life' through the gap and then the door started to close again.

I put my foot in the way.
"What do you want?" Shouted Lynne.
Ann stepped back and Lynne took her place in the doorway with her hand on her hip.
"I've come to get my stuff"
"After what you've done?"
"I haven't done anything! I just want to come in and get my stuff".
Lynne clocked Rachel recording on her phone and stepped back into the shadows but keeping her bodyweight on the door and her arm blocking the entrance.

"Ann's on the phone to the police" she said.

"That's good" Rachel said calmly.

Lynne seemed surprised at that response and the weight behind the door seemed to slacken a little. I took my opportunity and ducked underneath her arm and into the small hallway. There was a yell as Ann bounded up the stairs of the 3–storey home and Lynne tried to push me back towards the door. She seemed to realise that she wasn't going to have the strength to get me out so changed tactic 360 degrees and instead slammed the door shut and deadlocked it so that I couldn't get out. I paused, a little confused but made the decision to carry on with the task in hand. I dove into Skyla's room, which was on the ground floor of the two and half storey house and started shoving her clothes into a bag. Lynne blocked that door with her body, and I could hear Ann on the phone to the police. "He forced his way in" I heard.

Lynne shouted, "And I want him done for assault". The bedroom window was open, and I heard Rachel chuckle outside.

"Don't worry, she said through the window, I'm still recording.".

I grabbed a big bag of nappies and the bag I had just filled and shoved them out of the window. Next, my stuff. I dodged past Lynne again and shot to the top floor to our bedroom and saw that my stuff was already shoved into bin bags. I grabbed the bags and headed back down the stairs intending to shove those out of the window too.

"Mum's locked him in" I heard Ann say. Then "Mum, they said to unlock the door and let him out".

I glared at Lynne.

"Fine" she muttered and took the key out of her pocket, unlocked it, and opened the door wide.

I stepped through it.

My dad was also on the phone to the police. They had called him as Rachel had given his telephone number as a point of contact when she made the request for their help earlier. He was calmly explaining what was going on from his point of view on the other side of the door.

Rachel and I loaded my belongings into the two cars and then we heard the sirens. The police were on their way, just as we had predicted, only now it was as a 999 call rather than an assistance call. Oh well! Dad said to go home with Rachel, and he would speak to them as he felt that having me there any longer might just inflame the situation more.

We got home and waited. Sure, enough around an hour later the police turned up to my parents' house. Again, we invited them in and tried to explain the whole sorry situation.

The male officer seemed sympathetic.

"Look" he said. "It's clearly a domestic, but you really need to not go round there again".

"I don't want to" I replied, "but I've still got stuff of mine there, like a TV and stuff". He advised that I either go through the courts or ask somebody to go and collect the stuff on my behalf. He claimed that Ann didn't mind somebody else going but she didn't want to see me, and she wanted her key back.

He also told me that Lynne had raised a complaint of assault. Could this get any worse?

"Try not to worry" he said kindly. "Just stay away and try to get things resolved amicably but if you can't, do it properly through the legal channels".

I assured him I would.

"I'm going to Citizens Advice tomorrow" I told him. There was absolutely no mention of Skyla and when I checked the bag that she had passed to me earlier, it was full of Skyla's clothes.

Later, reading the police disclosure report it turned out that Ann had made another call to the police before I had arrived but after she had been to my parents' house. It reads:

3rd November 11:48 – Caller is trying to see her daughter, but he won't let the caller even hold.
Daughter is Skyla Organ. He took her to see grandparents and didn't bring her back. He is Carl Organ. The caller states that he has depression.
Caller states that she wants the police to deal with this. She says she wants Social Services told about this.
I have googled the number and passed this to the caller.

The caller is reporting that her ex-partner has their daughter, but

she would like her back. There is no court order in place and it's
not for the police to intervene in these circumstances.
I have reviewed the linked incident from yesterday where the
caller made allegations regarding her ex-partner. Police attended
overnight (less than 12 hours ago), checked on Skyla and were
happy to leave her with her father and his family.
There is no further requirement to attend based upon this call.
The caller has been provided with the number for Social Services
if she wishes to raise any matters with them.
This will be closed.

It had been a hell of a day. I held Skyla close.
"Don't worry" I whispered in her ear. "Daddy's going to make
everything right".

The next few days passed in a bit of a blur of Citizens Advice, letter writing and solicitors. Citizens Advice told me that before I could do anything, I had to go through a mediation service. This was basically a mechanism that the system hoped would resolve matters between parties before utilising the already over-worked court system. We had to find a registered mediator and pay for it. They would engage with Ann, but if she refused to resolve matters through them, they would issue a 'certificate' that allowed me to ask the Family Court to help. I looked through the mediators in my local area and contacted one at random.

It was pretty painless, and she reassured me that she would contact Ann and invite her to talk. I stressed that my only focus was making sure that contact with Skyla was fair. I was confident that Ann would take the mediation route, after all she must be desperate to see her baby by now. It had been nearly a week. I had tried to call her several times, but my calls went unanswered. I sent a couple of text messages and asked if she would like to at least 'video call' with me so that I could put Skyla on, but again, no response.

You must remember that at this point I was heartbroken. One minute I was in a committed relationship with talks of marriage and the next I was single, branded a child abuser and back in my old bedroom at my parents. I was doing my best to care for my baby daughter and mend my broken heart at the same time.

Despite the broken heart and the drama that had unfolded with no warning, I had to continue with my life for the sake of Skyla. She was my reason for getting up in the morning. Christmas was coming and I took Skyla to see the lights being switched on in the Market Place. We were walking to the centre when I spotted Ann and Lynne walking straight towards me. She was pushing Tammie in Skyla's push chair while Tiffany walked alongside

I braced myself. What would she do? Try to grab Skyla? I tightened my grip on the borrowed buggy that I was pushing. But to my surprise, they both deliberately looked away and rushed past me. They hadn't even attempted to look at Skyla. I was surprised. I knew that if it was me, I would have been desperate for even a glimpse of my baby.

The following week I was contacted by the mediator. To my surprise Ann had refused to co-operate in any kind of mediation and the following day I received a letter from a solicitor in Cirencester. It stated that I must hand Skyla to her mother immediately or court action would be taken. With it were a bundle of legal aid forms that I assumed meant to demonstrate that he meant business. It was the step I had been waiting for as now I would receive the 'Certificate' from the mediator, and I could focus my attention on finding a solicitor with the help of my nan.

There was only one solicitor who worked with "Legal Aid" in Cirencester and Ann had already appointed them so I had to look further afield.

I found a solicitor in Swindon and my nan took me to see her the next day. It was a free initial consultation, and I was confident that because I was out of work that legal aid would be offered. There was no way I could afford solicitors fees, but it would all be OK I thought to myself. However, the next blow. Legal Aid is only available in family law cases where a parent is 'at risk' or who has suffered 'violence'. Of course, I had not. What on earth was I going to do? I couldn't afford a solicitor. And how the hell was Ann getting legal aid? I shuffled through the papers I had received from them and scanned through the legal aid forms that had been submitted to the court on Ann's behalf. And there it was. Yet another lie. There in the check box where it asked if there had been violence was a big tick.

"This is outrageous" I said. "How can she be getting legal aid with no evidence?" I knew there was no evidence of violence because there had been none!

Natalee, the solicitor I was in consultation with explained quietly that unfortunately, her word was enough in these cases. It just seemed so unfair.

"You don't actually need representation" said Natalee. "You can represent yourself".

"Too risky" said my nan, "That woman wouldn't know the truth if it jumped up and bit her and we all know who's side the court will take." She looked at me. "No", she said with a determined look. "You need someone to speak for you who knows what they are doing. Don't worry about the money, we will sort that out later".

I looked at Nan.

"Thank you" I said quietly. I was so grateful. Of course if I had to go it alone I absolutely would, but I wouldn't have a clue what I was doing and would no doubt be battered into submission by Ann's solicitor. I was much more comfortable with having someone who knew what they were doing represent me. Thank God for Nan.

We started the necessary paperwork with Natalee, and I had myself a solicitor.

Over the next couple of weeks, letters went flying back and forth between solicitors. I couldn't believe the depths that Ann was sinking to. She was claiming that I was violent, controlling, manipulative, mentally unwell and Lord knows what else. She had even managed to get a volunteer worker at a local community group to write a statement claiming that she had witnessed me shouting at Ann. I had never been anywhere near this group and had certainly never met this woman..

I absolutely agreed that Ann should have contact with Skyla and suggested that we organise this through a 'contact centre'. This was rejected by Ann, and she countered with the suggestion of spending time with Skyla on her own at the same community centre that had offered a witness statement in support of Ann. Natalee quickly responded that this was not a location that could offer a "non-biased" approach to the contact and gave my concerns that Ann would take Skyla and then refuse to attend the court hearing.

I was determined that this case would be resolved in court. I was going to do everything in my power to deter her from stopping me from seeing my daughter. You might argue that I was doing the same thing, but I honestly knew that if I handed Skyla over, I would never see her again. I knew that while I had Skyla in my custody, Ann would be forced to attend the court hearing and everything would be done legally.

I bore the brunt of a lot of criticism over this from people who would make remarks such as "a child belongs with her mother". I thought this was a bit sexist. Surely a child belongs with both parents? Why a mother over a father? But I also had a lot of support. The court had already notified CAFCASS , who in turn requested that Social Services pay me a visit and file a report to be seen by the court in the upcoming case.

I wasn't unduly concerned about the visit. I knew that Skyla was perfectly happy and content and was completely unaffected by what was going on around her. Why would she be? She was just nine months old and couldn't possibly understand that she was in the centre of a tug of war.

Two women arrived from social services, one of whom was Skyla's usual health visitor, Ms Carter. They were both amenable and just interested in making sure that Skyla was happy and healthy, which there was no question about. But then Ms Carter said something that took me totally by surprise.

"A child really is best placed with her mum" she said matter of factly.

"Why?" I asked curtly.

"Well, don't you think she is missing her sisters?" She asked.

"I'm missing her sisters", I told her "I'm not stopping them spending time with Skyla, OR Ann, but Ann hasn't once contacted me to even ask how Skyla is". I pointed out. My mum stepped in

"Have you got any concerns over Skyla's welfare?" She asked them both pointedly?

"Well, no, but…"

"Well then" Mum cut her off, "once the court has outlined the custody arrangements everything will be sorted, but until then, Ann can see Skyla in a contact centre or come here if she would like."

Both the officials looked uncomfortable, but they acknowledged that there were no concerns about Skyla's safety, and they would be outlining this in their report to CAFCASS.

The preliminary court date was set for the 23rd of December. This would be when the judge would hear the case for the first time and Natalee explained that it was unlikely that it would be resolved at this hearing but that he would set out evidence he wanted to see at a future hearing and of course he would say where Skyla should live until then and what, if any, visitation there should be from the "other" parent.

It was so close to Christmas, and I hoped with everything that I had that the judge would allow me to see my little girl on her first Christmas Day. I was a realist. I knew deep down that it was unlikely that a judge was going to side with a father, and I was certain that he would ask me to return Skyla to her mother. Natalee agreed that it was the likely outcome but assured me that she would do her best to make sure that I got to see Skyla as often as possible.

Unfortunately, Natalee was unavailable to attend the court hearing herself, so she arranged for a barrister to represent me in her absence. I had received the papers that were being presented to the court the day before. I was gobsmacked. Some of the things that were being said were just down-right lies. You would have thought I should have expected that, but what I didn't expect was that she had managed to convince others to write witness statements supporting her allegations.

Possibly the lowest blow was the statement from Ann's doctor's surgery. In it the Dr claimed that she had questioned Tiffany about what she had seen, and Tiffany had confirmed to her that I had smacked Skyla. Reading it was painful. I had never laid a finger on any child, and I had certainly never smacked a tiny baby.

I wondered if it had taken long to prep Tiffany for this appointment. I was also fully aware that "mud sticks." Was I now going to be branded some kind of child abuser? I just hoped that the fact that the police had attended and were perfectly happy to leave Skyla with me would be evidence enough that this allegation was just nonsense and had been used for the sole purpose of punishing me.

I was already aware that the volunteer from the community project wrote a scathing account of my "manipulating coercive control". "Domestic abuse" "display of aggression" the list went on. I had never met the woman. I voiced my concern to Natalee that her 'testimony' would be believed as she was a 'professional' and she just shrugged it off.

"Don't worry Carl, it clearly says in her statement when she describes all of this behaviour that it is behaviour that she has been "told" about." She smiled. "She has only been told about it so the judge will throw it out, this witness statement is not a witness at all."

I breathed a sigh of relief.

In addition, Natalee received an email from Ann's solicitor out of the blue stating that she believed that I wasn't Skyla's father and had no paternal rights whatsoever. It went on to invite me to bear half the cost of a DNA test.

"Will you pay half?" Natalee asked.

"No" I said. "There has never been any doubt that I am her dad".

"Well, it's quite strange that she is only mentioning this possibility now" she agreed.

She responded to her solicitor that there was no need, and we never received a response on that subject, and it never came up again.

The morning of the first hearing arrived. My nan was driving me to the court in Gloucester. I got dressed in a shirt and tie and stood in front of the mirror. Deep breath. "Everything is going to be OK" I said to myself.

The drive to the court seemed to take forever. Possible outcomes going over and over in my mind and me rehearsing my reaction to every eventuality. I imagined that I would stand in front of a judge, but it was nothing like that.

I met with my barrister, and we went into a room on our own. He had already received all the background information and we sat and chatted about what had happened and what I hoped the outcome of today would be.

"What do you want, Carl?" He asked.

"Well, I want 50/50 custody I replied firmly".

"Only 50/50?"

"Well, no, I'd quite like Skyla to live with me and visits with Ann" I said, but I'll never get that".

"Well let's start high and let them beat us down to the 50/50" he said with a smile.

Ann and I were kept in separate rooms with my barrister hopping between the two to discuss 'proposals' and 'counter proposals'. Finally, the judge was ready to make his decision.

Skyla would stay with ME!! Dates were set out when Ann could spend time with Skyla and the idea of a contact centre was rejected, Ann could take Skyla without supervision, but dates and times were clearly set out. As it was Christmas, Ann was also to have 2 hours with Skyla on Christmas Day and on Boxing Day, but other than that, she would have her for 6 hours a week until the Directions hearing which had been set for the 22nd of January 2020. There was no provision for overnight stays. I was to be the primary caregiver to Skyla.

Wow, my barrister had done a blinding job. I hadn't dared hope for such an outcome and couldn't control my excitement.
"Thank you so much" I told him.
"You are very welcome" he said with a smile "Merry Christmas".

The drive back to Cirencester was spent making hands free calls to Mum, Dad, Ash, Rachel. Everyone was over the moon. This was the best possible outcome. It was going to be a Merry Christmas indeed.

Christmas 2020

Skyla's first visit to Ann was Christmas Eve. I was incredibly nervous. It had been agreed that I would meet Ann at a patch of ground close to the home we had once shared for the "hand-over" and I was dreading it. In all the time since the beginning of November, Ann had refused to let me have anything of Skyla's, so I was still without a pushchair. I had purchased a cot, but funds were extremely limited to me. Not least because my benefits had always been paid into Ann's account (something she had convinced me was a great idea as she was better with finances than me!) and so it had taken a while for me to sort out the changes.

Ann had also refused to give me any of the child benefit she received for Skyla, so money was extremely tight. I was in the process of applying for the child benefit, but Ann had obstructed this move by refusing to admit that Skyla did not live with her and therefore I had been forced to wait for court paperwork to send off with my claim.

I dressed Skyla up nice and warm and cuddled her close as I carried her the short walk to the "hand over" point. I arrived at the green, but Ann wasn't there yet. The location could be seen from her kitchen window, so I assumed she was staying in the warm until she could see I was there. I waited anxiously until she appeared from her front door. I braced myself chanting to myself "stay calm, stay calm".

Just like she had in my mum and dad's living room on the 3rd of November, she didn't say a word. Refused even to make eye contact and just opened her arms in a gesture for me to hand Skyla to her.

"She's had some breakfast and has a clean nappy on" I said nervously as I handed her over.
Nothing.
She took her roughly from me, and practically ran back to the house slamming the door behind her. I don't really know why I had expected anything else, but there it was.

"Don't worry" my mum said when I told her about it when I got home, "Things will settle into a routine and get easier" she reassured me.

I spent the entire four hours fretting about whether she was going to adhere to the Court Directions and bring her back to me at 4:00pm as arranged. Ann had blocked me on Facebook, but Lynne seemed to want to rub my nose in it. "My grandchildren all together" her profile read. A picture of the three girls together. I couldn't help but notice that Skyla had been changed out of the clothes I had put her in that morning.

Lynne had also updated her personal "bio" information so that it now included the names of all three girls rather than just Tammie and Tiffany. I was pretty pissed off to read that she had printed Tiffany and Tammie's full names but called Skyla "Skyla Green" rather than her proper name. It was petty and I knew that it had been done for effect and I vowed to ignore it.

There were also new pictures of Mike spending time with Tammie and Tiffany. Although there were no 'family' photos that included Ann the images clearly showed that despite the Restraining Order, Mike was now back in their lives. It shouldn't have bothered me, after all I absolutely agreed that a father should be part of a child's life, but I did worry that this 'violent' man that Ann had told me all about was going to be spending time with Skyla.

Thankfully, when I arrived at the "hand-over" location at 4:00pm, Ann appeared from her front door and marched over with Skyla in her arms. Skyla was again dressed in the clothes I had dressed her in that morning which made me chuckle. Ann held Skyla out to me.

"Hey Princess" I said and gave her a kiss in greeting.

Ann turned and started to walk away without a word again.

"Ann" I called "Can I use the pushchair?" Nothing. She carried on walking.

And that's how it was for every handover. Ann refused to communicate with me in any way at all.

"It's ridiculous" I said to Nan. "I get her back and I have no idea if she has on a clean nappy, if she has eaten, nothing".

I was concerned that vital information about Skyla was going to be left unsaid, purely because Ann couldn't bring herself to even look at me, so I asked Natalee to write to her solicitor again. We proposed that we keep a book that stayed with Skyla for her handovers that contained important information so that I could at least know if she had eaten. Her solicitor confirmed that she would fill out the book. It was a ridiculous situation, but my only concern was Skyla and hoped that eventually Ann would get over her "strop" and start to at least be civil.

The Directions hearing on the 22nd of January had finally arrived. After the success of the interim hearing, I was feeling much more confident, but there was still that element of doubt at what might happen.

Natalee was representing me again. We had been working hard together to disprove all the allegations that Ann had made about me. We had also put together a pretty strong case of our own to prove that Ann struggled as a single parent to three small children and that having me play more than a "visiting father" role in her life was in Skyla's best interests.

We were able to disprove her allegations that I was suffering from a mental illness with evidence from my GP. We also countered that Ann WAS suffering with mental issues, evidenced in her application and interview for a Personal Independence Payment award based on her mental health and need for help with everyday tasks because of it.

The evidence of the Community Project Volunteer was not heard as it provided no real insight as Natalee had predicted. The judge listened to both sides and then ruled. "Shared custody". Fantastic. I was going to have equal parenting rights to my baby. You must remember, all of this happened so quickly. One minute I was dreaming of a happy family, the next just fighting to be able to be a father to my daughter. And now it was over. I wasn't going to get my "Happy Ever After" with Ann, but now I had a new future. Not the one I had dreamed of, but it was more than enough for me. I was going to throw myself into being the best Dad I could be to Skyla.

Next was the issue of handovers. Natalee argued that it wasn't entirely fair that I should "deliver" and "collect" each time and that it should be an equal distance for both of us. It was suggested that each parent collect from the others home address. That seemed fair to me but was rejected by Ann. We tried the other way around, but again it was rejected.

"It's too confusing". She argued. "It should be the same place every time".

Natalee played a blinder. "Fine, in that case we will change it to the green outside Mr Organ's home, is that OK?"

Ann looked flustered.

"Um well, fine". She said looking blind-sided.

The colour was rising from her chest as realisation at what had just happened dawned on her. She glared furiously at her solicitor.

"That's settled then" said the Judge "I will arrange for an Order to be drawn up outlining the shared custody arrangements".

That was that. The custody was to be a 50/50 split starting immediately and would follow a pattern of 2 nights with me, 2 nights with Ann, 3 nights with me, etc. I was satisfied and could even put up with Ann's sulks during the handovers. It was done. Everything was set in stone by a court. I was still seething that her lies had allowed her to receive legal representation without paying a penny, but I reasoned that you get what you pay for, and in this instance, paying for my solicitor had actually been worth every penny.

I prepared myself for my new routine and restarted my job-hunt. I had put everything on hold as I had no idea what my circumstances were going to be. Now everything was sorted, I felt I could start working again.

Ann would only communicate via text or letter which was a pain, and she was being deliberately awkward about anything and everything. She had stopped my application for the child allowance and insisted on putting it in herself. She was clearly unhappy at the thought of me receiving any money directly. I received a message from Ann telling me that she had filled in the forms and that when I handed Skyla back next, I should just sign them

It didn't make any sense to me. Ann was already in receipt of Family Allowance for 2 children. The payment for the first child was a higher amount than payments for additional children which meant that if I claimed the allowance for Skyla as the parent of only one child, I would receive the higher amount. As this money would need to be split equally between both of us it made much more sense for me to make the claim.

It was clear that this was the way it was going to be from now on, but I couldn't let Ann's continual sulks put a dampener on the fact that I had been awarded shared custody. I didn't think it was ever going to be easy, but I hoped things would improve time went on.

The End? I know what you are thinking. Well, that was a pointless book. Nothing millions of other blokes haven't been through. In fact, you're thinking I'm the lucky one. So many others don't get a chance to see their kids at all. What a waste of reading time that was! But wait. I'm not finished. This is where the story REALLY starts. Sorry for the long prelude but you really did need to know the background stuff first. Keep reading. I promise, it's NOT your average "Father overcomes" story.

Two weeks passed and Skyla's first Birthday was in just two days' time. The handovers had been predictable. Nothing had changed except the location. Ann was still sullen and refused to even look at me.

The court order stated that on significant days such as Skyla's Birthday, the order would be varied as follows:

On Skyla's birthday she will spend 2 hours in the afternoon with the parent she is not with on that day

The schedule meant that Skyla woke up on her first birthday with Ann, but then she should be returned to me at 10:00am and I was so excited. We had planned a big party with all the family to celebrate. It was to be a celebration of not just her birthday, but that we had come through the last few months despite the lies. There was a lot to celebrate. Only it didn't quite go that way.

The day before Skyla's birthday a letter dropped onto my door mat. It was hand delivered but I never saw who delivered it. Addressed to myself, I noted the name of Ann's solicitor on the envelope. Curious I opened it. As I read it, I felt like I had been punched in the gut. I sank down onto the sofa.

"What's wrong?" My mum asked. I silently handed her the letter. Mum started to read it and burst into tears.
"It's not true" I said firmly.
Mum looked at me and said
"`Who the hell is Dan Jones?"

The letter from the solicitors stated in very simple terms, Ann had carried out a DNA test on another man and it is proven that Dan Jones is in fact Skyla's father. She won't be bringing her back.

I couldn't breathe. Enclosed with the letter were the results of the DNA test and there in black and white in amongst all these weird numbers were the words **99.9% *conclusive that Dan Jones is the biological father of Skyla Organ.***

I don't recall much more of that day. My heart had been broken into a million pieces. It couldn't be true, I thought to myself. It just couldn't. But there it was.

And if she thought I wasn't Skyla's father, why hadn't she pushed it during the custody hearings? I know her solicitor had mentioned it in a letter, but it had never been pursued. If she had just told the Court that I might not be her father, they would have stopped everything while they waited for a DNA test! What was her game? Had she hoped that she would win custody and then her dirty little secret would never be revealed, and I would carry on thinking that I was her father but never get to see her? I just didn't understand what the hell was going on. Nothing made sense. I was broken.

My nan came straight round.
"Well she can't just NOT bring her back" she said. "It's still a court order, I've made an appointment to see Natalee".
"Is there any point?" I asked.
"Don't you give up now Carl" she warned – look at that DNA test and tell me you think that's real?" I looked from Nan to the paperwork on the table. I had already thought to myself that it didn't look 'right' but what did I know about DNA tests? And surely, I only thought that because it was what I wanted to believe, but now Nan was saying it too.
"It doesn't look right, does it?" I asked her hopefully.
"No – It does not" she said.

The following day, my little girls first Birthday came, and I spent the afternoon in my solicitor's office instead of at the Birthday party I had planned.

"Well, it certainly doesn't look very professional" agreed Natalee.
She turned to her computer and started tapping away.
"Look" she said. "Even the company name, NorthGene Limited" is spelt in three different ways.
She glanced from the computer to the pages and back again.

"No" she affirmed, "something is not right".

"So, I can get her back?" I asked.

"Well," Natalee said, she has broken the court order, but I can't make her bring her back to you. I will apply to the Court for an urgent hearing again and we will ask for a legal DNA test".

"How long with THAT take" I asked.

Natalee looked at me. "I don't know Carl; it might take a while I'm afraid".

My heart was breaking but there was nothing I could do but wait until the next court hearing. I couldn't believe that her solicitor had actually advocated that she breaks the court order. Surely that wasn't something he should do? Surely, he should have done the right thing and applied to the court for an amendment to the order? So many questions about how this had happened were running through my mind but most importantly "was she actually mine?". I knew the answer. She WAS mine. I was absolutely sure of it.

I even contacted this NorthGene company. I sent them the report that I had received and the replied explaining that they couldn't give me any information regarding clients, however, they could confirm that any test results compiled by them would not take this form. They also sent me a copy of what a DNA test result paper would look like if it had been sent by them.

More proof. This DNA test was a fake and there was nobody in the world that could convince me otherwise.

"Come on Carl" my dad said. "I know you WANT her to be yours, and she might be, but the fact is that this other bloke MUST have slept with Ann for him to agree to take a bloody test".

"Maybe he's in on it?" I said hopefully. There were so many scenarios going through my head.

Dan Jones didn't exist, and it was a fake test?

Dan Jones DID exist, and they had used a child of his to fake the test?

Dan Jones DID exist and now thought he was the father, but Ann had faked the results?

I lost count of the different ways I thought of that could have resulted in the result that was printed on that piece of paper. But after my initial shock, not once did I contemplate that the results were genuine.

That wait for the urgent court hearing was torture. I had to wait a full month before the case was heard and, in that time, Skyla was hidden from me. All photographs were removed from social media and her name has been changed again on both Ann and Lynne's Bio's. She was now known as Skyla Jones, and I was being erased from her life.

During my wait I did everything I could to find out who he was, but nobody seemed to know anything about him. I stalked his Facebook profile and saw that he was father to two other children but estranged from their mother. I couldn't remember ever hearing his name before and we only shared one mutual friend. That's quite rare in our small town, but then he was a little older than me.

If he HAD been sleeping with Ann it certainly hadn't been a relationship as he appeared nowhere in her Facebook feeds, so I convinced myself that he was a friend of both Ann and Lynne, and this was some bizarre deception they had cooked up between themselves. My theory seemed to make even more sense with Lynne's continued Facebook updates which seemed to be pushing Dan as part of her family. The feelings of anger I felt when reading her updates. There were never any pictures, just text "Such a lovely afternoon with Skyla and her daddy". And "Skyla spent a lovely time with her daddy today". Each time Dan was tagged, showing that he was a Facebook "friend" and now very much part of her family. I swear, I wouldn't have been responsible for my actions if I had been within 10 feet of her. It felt like deliberate messages composed with the aim of winding me up.

"Don't bite" everyone warned. "If you do anything, it will give them the 'evidence' that they never had that you are violent". I knew they were right, but my God!

The Court date was set for 9th March. Natalee had already warned me that I was unlikely to be allowed to see Skyla until paternity had been established. This just didn't seem fair to me. It now seemed that the tables had truly turned and despite the lies and deceit the whole system was now in Ann's favour. I would not be allowed to see my daughter until I proved I was her father. It no longer mattered that I had watched her come into the world, loved, and cherished her. Fought tooth and nail for her. Nobody cared about that anymore.

The morning of 9th March arrived and here I was again, donning my smartest trousers, shirt, and tie. I posted a picture on Facebook titled "Dressed for war". I was ready.

Again, my nan drove me to Gloucester Court and again I sat and listened to a fresh new set of lies. This hearing was no longer focussing on the lies about my being a terrible person and an unfit father. Now the court was being asked to believe a few scraps of paper with random numbers scattered all over the pages meant that I should be discharged of my parental rights. You heard me. Ann had made an application to have my name removed from Skyla's birth certificate. My heart sank.

Natalee immediately argued that the DNA test that had been carried out without proper checks should be ignored and that a legal and procedurally correct DNA test be ordered. The judge, a woman this time, did enquire of Ann why she had not mentioned during the previous hearings that there was doubt as to the paternity of Skyla and she just shrugged her shoulders.

Through Natalee, I had made an application to have the original Court Order custody arrangement reinstated. I knew it was a long shot, but she gave it everything she had, even managing to slip into the court about 'Dan Jones' spending time with Skyla. The judge did not look happy at all. Turning to Ann she asked politely.
"How well do you know this man, Miss Green?"
"Well, um." Ann stuttered.
The judge didn't wait for a reply, just gave a disdainful look that made it perfectly obvious that she didn't approve. Nevertheless, the judge also didn't agree that it was in Skyla's best interest to allow me to have access to her while her paternity was in question. I felt deflated, but I was promised that the DNA test would be carried out as quickly as possible. I was back to waiting. Waiting and staring at the empty cot in my bedroom back in my parents' house.

The DNA tests were ordered to be arranged and that the results should be sent to the court in time for the next hearing on the 5th of May. 5th MAY. Natalee tried to reassure me that the tests would be conducted, and the results would be sent well ahead of the 5th of May. The advantage of this would be that if it showed that I was NOT Skyla's father, the 5th of May date would be irrelevant as I would offer no objections to the discharge of my paternal rights and if it showed that I WAS her father, well the date was already set, and I could look forward to having the custody arrangements reinstated.

The next few weeks I slipped further and further back into the darkness. Where gym and exercise had been my release, now that I was unemployed, I could no longer afford the membership fees. Besides which, I had no desire to do anything. Getting out of bed was a real achievement for me these days. If I did manage to get out of bed it was only to either, make my way to the living room sofa or to the nearest pub.

I suppose it was fortunate that I was so skint, otherwise I think I may have managed to develop a drink problem. Every day was now the same. Just waiting for a letter or email telling me when the DNA test was going to happen. Progress was further marred due to the Corona Virus Pandemic that was gaining momentum across the world and because of it everything was 1000 times harder to arrange.

Finally, arrangements were made for somebody from the DNA testing company to come to the house to take a sample from me. I was relieved as the Government had now imposed a legal lock-down and only essential work was permitted. Fortunately, Court Orders are most definitely seen as essential so although things didn't happen as fast as they might normally, they did happen.

A man from DNA Legal arrived late March with a briefcase full of paperwork and testing kits. It was all very quick and easy. We went through the usual identification verification process by confirming my name and date of birth. I then produced my passport to further verify who I was. The man passed me two long cotton-bud type sticks and told me to scrape them on the inside of my cheek for a full minute. It wasn't an unpleasant experience but felt quite awkward with a bloke standing there staring at me. Finally, I posed for a photograph that would be included in the report.

Once it was done, I placed the swabs into the bag he had given to me. And that was that.

"Are you going to Ann Green next"? I asked.

He looked at me blankly.

"Ann Green, to get a test from Skyla". I pressed.

"Oh, no, sorry" he replied, "I only have you on my list today".

I felt disappointed. I had hoped that being in the same area, we might be done on the same day, but of course, due to 'confidentiality' there was no way of me finding out when Skyla would have her test. Or if she had already had it.

Waiting, waiting, waiting. My life was on hold. I was still job hunting, but I'll be honest, it was no longer with as much effort as there should have been. Life was dark. We were in the middle of a Global Pandemic, everybody was pretty much on house arrest with only 1 hour of exercise recommended so there seemed to be nothing to look forward to. I couldn't go anywhere or do anything to even attempt to take my mind off Skyla. She was all I could think about, and it was torture. Was she OK? Was she being cared for properly? Did she miss me?

The results were going to go straight to Natalee, and she had promised that she would let me know the minute they came in. And around 4:30pm on Friday 17th April I received an email from Natalee.

I don't even remember how it was worded now as the only words that mattered were the ones that shattered my world.

.. I'm sorry Carl, you are not the father. That same feeling I had when that letter had dropped onto my doormat back in February. Utter devastation. I'm not ashamed to admit it. I sobbed my heart out. I didn't even know how to tell everyone, so I just muttered it to Mum and Dad and then went back to my room and shut the world out. The country was in lock down so I couldn't even go to the pub to drown my sorrows, which in hindsight was probably a good thing. I just lay on my bed, staring at the ceiling trying to choke back the tears.

I scrolled through my photos on my phone, reliving my happy memories. Memories of when I was a daddy. Everything had been taken from me. That dirty bitch had been cheating on me and I had no idea. Had she known all along that I wasn't the dad? Nah, she couldn't have done, else she wouldn't have waited to spring it on me like this. She would have told the police that very first night she made the allegations about me hurting Skyla. She had only had to say that I wasn't her father, and they would have taken her from me there and then.

Even later, during the custody arrangements. If she had brought it up in court, they would have ordered a DNA test then and all of this would have been done in December or January. I know that she had mentioned it back in November, but she certainly hadn't pursued it. Why? None of it made sense. Had she hoped that I would just lose custody and then her dirty little secret would never be exposed?

Clearly Ann and Lynne were in full victory mode. "Best news ever!" I read on Lynne's Facebook profile. I scanned down the list of congratulations messages from Ann's friends, each one feeling like I had a knife in my gut, and it was slowly being twisted.

I noticed my "notifications" icon flashing on Facebook and clicked on it. There I saw I was tagged into a Facebook Mike had written. It was actually a message direct to me.
"Dearest Carl Organ", it started. It went on to mock me stating "turns out you aren't even a father". That hurt.

As I lay there flicking through my phone, yet another notification popped up of a new email. It was another email from Natalee. This time she had attached the DNA test paperwork. "Great" I thought to myself. "I get to see it again". I scrolled through the pages of the test results.

We had been right to assume that the NorthGene results that had first come through were suspicious. The results papers form DNA Legal were completely different. Rather than sporadic numbers and letters scattered all over the pages, they were laid out neatly in a table. The DNA marker codes listed on the left. Then my DNA markers in the second column, followed by Skyla's markers in the third column.

The figures meant nothing to me. Why would they? The only important part of that test was the bottom line. That line that said very clearly 'Carl Raymond Organ is excluded from being the biological Father of Skyla Harris Organ'. My heart lost another piece. I scrolled down further. As with my own test, the representative from DNA Legal that visited Ann to take the sample from Skyla had been instructed to take a photograph.

I stared at the photograph. I stared harder. What the fuck! My heart leapt and I ran downstairs. Mum and Dad were sat watching TV. I shoved the photograph under my dad's nose.
"Who's that?" I asked.
Dad picked up the paper and peered at the photo.
"I don't know" he said, "who is it?".
"It's supposed to be Skyla" I told him.
Dad looked at me, clearly confused.
"What"?
"It's supposed to be Skyla" I said again, almost shouting.

The picture in the report showed a small child wrapped tightly in a blue blanket with a dummy in her mouth. The face of the child looked confused, but most importantly, there was a large amount of hair poking out from under the blanket. Skyla didn't have any hair. She was one of those babies that was born with no hair at all and any hair that she had grown since was so fine and blonde that it would be easy to forgive you for thinking there was none there at all. I know I hadn't seen her in 10 weeks, but I failed to see how she could have grown the thick fringe that was clearly on display in this photo.

I couldn't say for sure who the child was, although it did resemble Tammie, but it sure the hell wasn't Skyla. I didn't think I could cope with this rollercoaster of emotions I was experiencing. First the suspect DNA results that landed on my mat, now this. It was Friday night and there was nothing I could do about it. I just prayed that Natalee was yet to inform the court that I would agree to have my name removed from her birth certificate. I would agree to no such thing!

I kept staring at the photograph. I started forwarding it to various relatives with no message attached. Each time the message would be replied with a simple "who's that?" I wasn't going mad. Nobody recognised that child as Skyla.

I couldn't wait until Monday and started composing an email to Natalee. Would she believe me? Rachel got together various photos of Skyla and of Tammie and she enlarged them on her computer. Her husband, my uncle Al is a keen photographer and has some great software and a great eye for detail. I valued his opinion, and he needed no convincing. He hadn't really met Skyla previously, so Rachel just gave him some photos along with the photo of the child in the DNA photograph. He didn't even have to enlarge it.

"That's not the same child" he said matter of factly.

"Are you sure?" Rachel asked him.

"Positive, look", he zoomed in on the one eye of both the DNA photo and of a photo of Skyla taken from roughly the same angle.

"Look at her eyebrows". He then pulled up a photo of Tammie and enlarged it to the same size and put them side by side. "And look at that". "Look at the outline of the shape. That eyebrow belongs to THAT child". He was pointing at the photograph of Tammie. He agreed with me, that was Tammie and not Skyla.

I opened the draft email that I had started to Natalee and attached the enlarged images hoping that the close-ups would add weight to my "story". Because who on earth was going to believe this? I couldn't believe it. Would Ann really try to fake a legal DNA test. Clearly the answer was yes, but how would I prove it? It was a long wait for Monday and a response to my email to Natalee.

On Monday I did receive a response and I can't say that the wording of it convinced me that she believed me, but the important part was that she was sure that the "identification" photograph that had been taken as part of the DNA test was not adequate for identification purposes.

It was also impossible to match the DNA marker figures with the figures that were printed on the NorthGene results that Ann had presented as a DNA test. They looked nothing alike, and this was something that Natalee pointed out to the court also.

We made an application to have the hearing that was scheduled for the 5th May delayed and asked for an order for another DNA test to be taken. Due to Covid there were no more trips to see a judge face to face. Everything was now being done by telephone and Natalee represented me at an urgent hearing. She outlined to the judge that the child in the photograph couldn't possibly be identified, and the judge agreed. I was a little annoyed that Natalee was taking this "path". I felt that she should be insisting that Ann had faked the test and to ask them to take this a little more seriously. I didn't see any reason why I couldn't be present for the DNA test, but my request was ignored. I felt like I wasn't being heard, but I supposed the important thing was that the DNA test was going to be repeated.

In addition, the court had ordered Ann to provide a statement outlining how and when she had paid for the DNA test with NorthGene and to present proof of payment.

The order was drawn up and this time the wording was very specific. The child must retake the test and a photograph must be taken with her head and face completely uncovered. I still couldn't see why I couldn't be a witness to the test, but not only was Ann still claiming that she was scared of me, the country was still in a national lockdown so COVID could be used as an ideal excuse for me not to be present.

This time the results were ordered to be with the court by the 12th of June. That would be four months since I had seen my little girl. Worse than that, the next available hearing date wasn't until the 30th of June. It felt like a lifetime away.

I didn't have to retake the test myself as my DNA Markers were already on file. I just had to wait patiently for Ann to make arrangements for the test to be "retaken". It was hard, but that belief that I was Skyla's dad was now even stronger. If she was using another child to take the test to make sure that it came back negative, then she MUST have something to hide I told anyone who would listen.

Everyone would nod kindly and just say "we just have to wait and see Carl". It really wound me up. Sometimes I thought that they didn't WANT me to be her dad.

"It's not that", Rachel said when I told her what I was thinking, "It's just that we don't want to see you disappointed again". She paused and looked like she was trying to find the right words for what she wanted to say next. "And you know, if Skyla IS yours, you are stuck with Ann in your life for years."

I didn't want to hear it. Nothing mattered except proving that Skyla was mine.

"And this Dan" she carried on. "Have you tried to contact him?"

"No, why?" I said.

"Well, if he DID take a DNA test then he must have slept with her at a time when Skyla COULD be his", she reasoned. "Otherwise, why else would he agree to do a DNA test in the first place".

"He's probably in on it" I said angrily.

"It's a possibility, but you should try and find out a bit more about him and his part in all this. At least, I would if I were you".

I thought about it. She was right, but I didn't think that he would talk to me and quite honestly, I didn't want to talk to him either. I spoke to Mum, and she agreed to try and contact him via Facebook Messenger. I sent a short message to him asking when he took the DNA test.

There was no immediate reply, but the following day he answered.

(Dan) *February*
(Mum) *Did you know she might be yours before then?*

(Dan) No, it was a complete shock. I had no idea until she asked me for test. So sorry. I cant imagine how you must all be feeling.

Well, that was something at least. It felt a bit better to know that he hadn't been part of a massive deception right from the beginning, but if she had thought that he might be the father that just made her even more evil. Deliberately keeping the fact that he might be the father from him for over a year and then just dropping it on him when it suited her to have him as the father rather than me now. My hatred for Ann just continued to grow with every day that passed.

Time dragged on and on waiting for the results. I didn't even know if the test had been taken so it just became a boring habit to pick up my phone every half hour to check for emails. In the meantime, Ann was clearly in hiding, or at least Skyla had been forced into hiding.

Because of the heavy fringe on the child in the photograph I think everyone in the family wanted to catch a glimpse of Skyla just to confirm that in 12 weeks or so she hadn't grown a full head of dark hair. Ridiculous, I know, but the situation was ridiculous, and you really start to doubt your own sanity when faced with such a ridiculous scenario.

But Skyla was nowhere to be found. She had been removed from Facebook. Where I had my suspicions that Lynne had deliberately posted pictures and statuses to mock me, she had now blocked me from her account and both Lynne and Ann had made their accounts 'private' which meant that if you were not a 'friend' you saw absolutely nothing when you searched their names.

Mutual friends told me that they had both conducted a Facebook cull and where they had once been "friends", they had now been removed and could see as much of their profile as I could. It seemed that they had both removed anybody who might support me.

Nobody had seen Skyla for weeks. On the few occasions that Ann was seen pushing a pushchair the hood was always pulled up and the seat had been rotated so that Skyla was always facing Ann. A close friend had a child the same age as Tiffany and they both went to the same nursery, and she reported that nobody could ever get a clear view of Skyla. Ever.

At around this time Ann moved home again. I imagine her reasons for moving were that she felt that her current address was far too close for comfort to my own. As I have explained before, Cirencester is a very small town, and it was amusing to discover that her new flat was directly opposite Jade's mum. Perfect, we thought, Sue, Jade's mum was bound to see her at some point. But no, each time Ann left the house with Skyla she was dressed in a pink woolly hat.

It was obvious that Ann was determined to hide her lack of hair. Not just from me, but it seemed from everybody. It seemed stupid. We would all know that she had used Tammie, for I was certain it was Tammie in the picture, for that first legal DNA test. Maybe she was hoping that the court would think that there had been an honest mistake on the first test, I thought. But still, we would be able to tell from the DNA markers that a different child had been used.

The 12th of June came and went. I emailed Natalee to enquire what was going on. The results should have been with the court by now, but like everyone else, Covid was having an impact on waiting time and so the results were late.

"It won't make any difference" Natalee said, if they are here in time for the hearing. But that wasn't the point. The most important thing to me was getting those results.

They arrived on the 15th of June. This time I didn't bother looking at the results straight away, I just wanted clarification that Skyla had been tested so I scrolled straight to the identification picture. And there she was. Tammie. This time there was absolutely no mistaking her. Sure, she had tried to disguise her again. Tammie was pictured with her face turned away from the camera and looked to be fast asleep. She also had her fringe and hair scraped back and covered by a thick headband, but those thick eyebrows were unmistakeable

Yet again, my heart sank. I got straight onto the phone to Natalee again.

"That's Tammie" I told her matter of factly. There was a long pause and Natalee cleared her throat.

"Are you sure Carl?" She asked.

"Absolutely positive" I insisted.

Another pause.

At that moment I knew that even my own Solicitor didn't believe me.

"I'm not sure that they will agree to order a THIRD DNA test she said, and if they do, they might ask you to pay for it".

I felt miserable.

"Look, I'll lay out in an email to you what you should do from here, when you should do it and how to approach various aspects, but I really don't think I can represent you any better than you can represent yourself from here".

I could have cried.

"OK" I said quietly and hung up.

Could things get any worse? As far as I was concerned that picture of Tammie was as plain as the nose on my face. So why were people turning the page this way and that to get a better look. Couldn't they see? Were they blind?

I could see that even my dad would sometimes have moments of doubt. This was a nightmare. What Ann was doing was illegal surely? She was in contempt of court at the very least. And at the bottom of both DNA Legal tests, she had presented Tammie for, she had signed a statement that said.

'I confirm that the information provided in this statement is true to the best of my knowledge and belief, and I make this statement knowing that, if it is tendered in Evidence, I shall be liable to prosecution if I have wilfully stated in it anything which I know to be false or do not believe to be true. [Criminal Justice Act 1967, s.9; M.C Act 1980, s.5A(3A) & 5B; M.C. Rules 1981, r.70]'

So why was nobody taking me seriously?

All I could do was throw myself into preparing to convince the Judge that the wrong child had been used. Again.

I put together a letter and included photos of Skyla and Tammie. I also pointed out that Ann had been ordered to ensure that Skyla be tested and that her head and face should be completely uncovered for the identification photograph, an order that she had ignored by placing a thick headband over Tammie's head.

In my letter I practically begged for another DNA test and asked to be witness. If I was there, it would be impossible for her to use Tammie, or any other child, instead of Skyla.

The evidence that Ann had been ordered to obtain to prove that the private DNA test was genuine arrived by email. This time the NorthGene report was completely different, it no longer looked like a scrambled mess of letters and numbers but was now similar to the DNA Legal results. She also presented a copy of a postal order in place of a receipt that she claimed she had used to make payment for the test. A postal order? Who pays with postal orders in 2020? I knew full well that Ann had a bank account and a debit card so to make the trip to the post office to purchase a postal order seemed very suspicious.

I studied the numbers, comparing the NorthGene test DNA markers for "Skyla" to those from the DNA Legal results. They did match. My head was scrambled. All that proved was that even IF she had done a genuine NorthGene test, she had used Tammie for that one too. But it was far more likely that she had used the DNA Legal results to make a more genuine template to present to the court.

In with all this paperwork that her solicitor had sent to me ahead of the hearing was Ann's arguments against having another DNA test.

'There can be no doubt that this sample was taken from Skyla and not Tammie' her solicitor, Richard, had written 'the mother would submit that it would be an abuse of Skyla to require her to submit to a third sample being taken'.

Also included was a formal application to have my parental rights discharged and my name removed from Skyla's birth certificate with immediate effect. My stomach turned over just reading the words. They really were trying to force this issue. All I could do at this point was hope with everything I had that the judge would see my photos. Surely once they saw those, they would HAVE to order another DNA test. Wouldn't they?

On the 30th of June the case was heard again. It was by telephone again. This time I had no representation, and I would have to speak for myself. Fortunately, the court had received my statement and evidence and while I know they didn't believe me either, it was pretty obvious that they didn't feel they could forcibly remove me as Skyla's father when there was still an element of doubt.

They ordered a "final" DNA test. The way they said "final" was a clear message that they would not be ordering a fourth. They also insisted that I pay for half. Ann was still in receipt of Legal Aid which infuriated me and so her half of the cost would be covered by the taxpayer. Dad had already reassured me that he would cover the cost of the test and quite frankly I would have found the money somewhere. There was no way I could give up now.

As I was paying for half of it, it stood to reason that I would be a witness to the test happening. But no, I tried to argue my case, but her solicitor was an old hand at this and managed to convince the judge that Ann would be too frightened in a room with me. It was decided that the test would take place with the health visitor, Ms Carter, acting as witness. I wasn't entirely happy with this, but nobody was listening. This time the results were ordered to be received by 11th August and the next hearing listed for the first available date after the 17th of August.

Another six weeks! That would be a full six months that I had been separated from my daughter.

The order stated that it was down to her solicitor to make the arrangements for the test. I'm not going to beat around the bush, the bloke was a bit of a cock. And not just because he was representing Ann. Ever since Natalee had stopped representing me the email correspondence about the case from him were just condescending and rude. It was clear that he now saw me as an easy target, and he felt that he could bully me into doing things his way.

It's hard to stand up for yourself in matters that you know next to nothing about against a bloke who deals with stuff like this for a living. He knew the jargon, who to write to and how things were 'supposed' to be done. I was just sending letters and emails left, right and centre hoping that somewhere along the line the right person would read it and take pity on me and forgive my lack of "procedure" and maybe point me in the right direction.

Around a week after the telephone hearing, I received a casual email from him stating that Ms Carter was unable to witness the test as she was on an extended period of absence. I laughed out loud as I carried on reading. He advised me that the test would now be witnessed by Sandra from the Churn Project. That would be the same volunteer that had written a witness statement for Ann accusing me of violence and coercive control. "I don't fucking think so" I muttered to myself. I quickly looked up the Court Order to get the correct wording and then shot back an email in reply:

Dear Richard

I do not agree to Sandra being present for the DNA test. I feel this would not be a suitable witness for various reasons, but most importantly that she has already presented herself as a witness for Ann and therefore cannot be independent.

I then listed 4 people I would be happy with. They included a teacher, 2 police officers and my uncle who is a warrant officer in the army. I also suggested that the test itself could be done at the Churn project location if Ann felt comfortable there.

His response appeared quite condescending

Dear Carl

Ann does not know any of these people and does not agree that they could identify Skyla. Sandra can make a positive identification. I will organise the test to be sent to the Churn Project asap, but you will need to call them today to arrange payment before they will send this.

His email really irritated me.
"Prick" I said out loud as I read it.

Dear Richard

I will not be paying anything until we agree on a suitable witness. I noticed that the court order says that if it is not possible for the health visitor to be present, the mother should apply back to the court, so I think we should probably do that and ask for them to give further direction.

This all resulted in yet another telephone hearing so that it could be decided how this test was going to be done and in front of who. MORE delay. I didn't like it, but again, I didn't stand much of a chance as the judge tended to direct everything at the only "legal" person in the call. It was infuriating but I was helpless to do anything about it.

It was now decided that the test would be taken at Ann's doctors surgery. Her solicitor had received an email from one of the doctors at the practice confirming that they were happy to host and witness the test. I objected. "I don't believe the doctor would be able to identify Skyla, I argued". "You never get to see the same doctor twice at that practice", but my objections were ignored, and a new order was created. The only good thing was that none of the deadline dates had been moved to consider the extra time it had taken to organise a venue and witness.

My hope was beginning to fade fast. How on earth could I be sure that they would test the right child?

"I have an idea," said Rachel. "Leave it with me".
About an hour later a document dropped into the 'Family Chat' group messages that we had created for this topic.
"Like it?" She typed into the group chat.
"Love it" both me and my nan said.
She had written a long letter addressed to each of the doctors at the surgery explaining the whole story and why it was so important they made sure that they took the sample from the correct child. It included pictures of Skyla and it outlined that the identification photograph must be a clear picture with nothing covering Skyla's head or face.

"Brilliant" typed my Nan. "I'll print them out and take them down to the surgery this afternoon". I felt a lot more confident. At least they would know the whole story and understand how important it was.

I received another email from Ann's solicitor prompting me to pay the fee, but as I read through the instructions that were to be sent with the test to the surgery, I noticed that there was no mention of the ID photograph.

Yet another email back to Richard politely pointing out that this needed to be included. When I received his reply, I was more than certain that he was deliberately trying to wind me up. He insisted that the Dr's identification would be enough and that a photograph wasn't necessary.

I wrote back

Dear Richard,

It's in the court order and I will not be paying for the test unless it is done properly. Please ensure that the doctor knows a photograph must be taken of the child that is tested.

The only reply I received was an update to the instructions. It was a big win for me, and I was SURE we had covered all angles. There was no way in the world that she could present Tammie for the test this time.

We were back to waiting and I had no idea when Ann was going for the test. It was now proving to be the hottest Summer for a long time, and Skyla was still being hidden from the world. Even taking her from her mother's car to her doorstep, she was made to wear a pink woolly hat. I was really starting to fret about her health and wellbeing. The poor child wasn't being given any opportunity to enjoy the sunshine at all.

We continued in vain our attempts to get a recent photograph of Skyla. It was no good presenting a six-month-old photo to the courts. Ann would just argue that her hair had grown and while we could argue that it was highly unlikely to have grown that much in those first hearings, six months had now passed, and we imagined that a court could easily be convinced that a baby's appearance changes a lot at that age. And hair does grow.

Our attempts would have been comical if the situation wasn't quite so tragic. There was an occasion when Ann was spotted walking with the pushchair towards town with an unknown woman. It was action stations all round. I was now working in a temporary role so could do nothing, but Ashley had been furloughed due to Covid and jumped in his car. As did my Nan. Our family chat group became a video chat as a group of desperate amateurs gave their best attempt at undercover surveillance. I don't think any of us will be looking for a career in MI5 anytime soon.

The pair of them drove into town and Ashely parked up and jumped into Nan's car. They continued their drive with Nan driving and Ashley keeping his eyes peeled for Ann and the pushchair. All the while the video chat was "live". Rachel and Jade were both working from their home offices and were barking ideas about where they could possibly be.
"Drive to the Tesco in town," said Rachel.
"No, go through the Market Place," shouted Jade.
"I can't bloody drive down there" Nan snapped.

They had pretty much driven down every street in town and the surrounding areas and had given up. Nan was driving Ashley back to his parked car when Ash spotted them.

"There she is" Ash said pointing out of the window, "Turn around, turn around".

"I can't turn around, I'm on a dual carriage-way".

"Shit" said Ash as he strained to turn around in his seat to keep his eye on her. "She went into Ciren Park". He shouted.

"Right, go to Cecily Hill and go in through the other entrance" shouted Rachel excitedly, "you can meet her coming the other way".

Nan drove towards Cecily Hill.

"There's nowhere to park!" I could hear the disappointment in her voice. She turned the car around again and headed back into town.

"Don't worry, she said I'll Park in Tesco and walk back up".

I was starting to worry now, my nan, while she still thinks of herself as a disco-dancing 20-year-old is a disabled, elderly woman).

"Be careful" I said, it's not worth hurting yourself for – Ash can't you run on back and get the shot".

"Don't worry about me" Nan said and then we got cut off.

I had no idea who the woman she was with was, but it was nice that they were taking a walk through the beautiful grounds of Cirencester Park with Skyla. It was a beautiful and hot summers day and I thought that the location had been chosen to give Skyla an opportunity to enjoy the sunshine with few people around. After all, it was a weekday and Cirencester Park, whilst quite popular was blessed with big wide-open spaces so it would be easy to find space well away from anyone else.

I waited anxiously for an update. Wondering if there had been any trouble or if they had managed to get a good picture. I had visions of my nan fronting up to Ann and telling her exactly what she thought of her and Ann reacting with her now polished victim act and immediately calling the police.

Around 40 minutes later the group video chat was restarted.

"Well?" We all said at once. "Did you get it?"

"No" Nan said sadly.

"What happened"?

"Nothing much, we had just got into the park, and she was right there walking towards us. She didn't notice us at first and Ash had his camera ready, but the pushchair had the hood up again facing away from us".

Ash took over "Yeah, I was going to walk straight past her and then turn quickly and get the picture of Skyla kind of like over her shoulder".

"So, what happened?" Jade asked impatiently

"She had the pink woolly hat on" he said with a sigh.

"What? It's 22 degrees out there" I said in disbelief.

My poor little girl was being treated like a bloody mushroom.

"Did you recognise the woman?" I asked.

Ash said no. "I got a photo of her though" he said proudly.

He sent the picture to the group chat, and I recognised her as a volunteer from one of these "Family Assistance" organisations. It's for families who are struggling, and they offer courses and counselling and stuff. I wondered what reason she could possibly have given to her as to why Skyla was being dressed in a woolly hat on one of the hottest days of the year!

This whole situation was starting to consume my every waking thought. I was more convinced than ever before that Skyla was mine, but with every passing day I grew more and more worried that I wouldn't be able to prove that Tammie was being used for the tests.

I felt sure that she was going to try to pull the same stunt again and could only hope that the doctors would catch her out. But then what would they do? She would tell them they were wrong. They would refuse to do the test, and then what?

We continued our quest to obtain that elusive picture of Skyla. I say picture, but at this point I think we would all have been happy just to catch a glimpse of her. There was no doubt that the child being used to take the DNA tests was Tammie, but when you are in the middle of a situation like this, you start to doubt your own name.

We deployed tactic after tactic. Sue, Jade's mum kept a log of when she left the house and returned and how, trying to establish if she had a routine. We kind of figured that she would walk to her mums on a Thursday at around 10 in the morning and return the same route at about 4:00pm. One swelteringly hot day in August, Rachel and my nan parked up on the route she must take to return home. Sue had confirmed she had left the flat as expected that morning, so they sat there for over an hour. Nothing! That day she decided to stay the night at her mothers. Disappointment again.

One Saturday morning, Sue spotted Dan chatting to Ann outside her flat. His car engine was running, and Ann had Skyla in her arms. Still with the pink woolly hat on. It looked very much as though he might be taking Skyla for a day out. Sue quickly grabbed her keys and ran to her own car ready to follow them.

She hoped that if Dan had Skyla on his own, she might be able to convince him to take a look at her and maybe even get a photo. Unfortunately, in the time it took to get to the car, Dan was already half way down the road and she was unable to catch him.

I couldn't help but chuckle as I pictured her jumping into her car and chasing him down the road.

Failed again, but we had everybody we knew on the lookout for her, and different updates would come back from various sources. She had a new boyfriend and despite lockdown regulations he started staying with Ann at her flat quite regularly. Lynne was also obviously keen to let me know about the new man in Ann's life as she temporarily lifted the tight privacy on her account. I started receiving messages from my friends with pictures showing me pictures of Ann and her new beau.
"I don't care" I would respond angrily
"Are there any pictures of my daughter?"

Of course, I DID care. Not that Ann was in a new relationship. I cared that yet another man was being introduced to Tammie and Tiffany, but more importantly MY daughter. Was this a new man to call daddy? How confused must those little girls be? And who was this new man in Skyla's life? Nobody seemed to know anything about him, so alongside trying to get sight of Skyla, I started looking into who he was.

Just a few days of discovering there was a new man on the scene, I received a message request from a woman I had never heard of. Intrigued I opened the message.

(Jenny) Do you know Ann Green? You her Ex?
   (Me) *Yeah, why*
(Jenny) *She's seeing my brother*
   (Me) *So?*
(Jenny) *Can you tell me anything about her?*
   (Me) *Tell your brother to run*
(Jenny) *He's changed since he met her. Something doesn't sit right with me about her*
   (Me) *She is hiding my daughter from me. She is dangerous. If your brother wants to know about her tell him to message me.*

Well at least I knew that someone looking out for this new bloke, but I doubted very much if he was going to want to listen to anything I had to say. I had no doubt that Ann would have created a fabulous story about me making herself the innocent victim. Just as she had done with Mike.

It was easy to find out more about the mystery man now that I knew his name. I was relieved to see that he had two daughters of his own that he was in regular contact with his children. He lived in Devon, and it appeared that they had "met" on TikTok. I had to laugh to myself as I watched the videos that they created and posted online badly lip-syncing to love songs. 'You poor deluded fool' I thought. That was me just 2 years ago, completely taken in by her lies. It was surprising just how bad she was at lip-syncing when you considered what an amazing actress, she had turned out to be.

It didn't take long for her to find the profile I had created on Tiktok for the purpose of tracking her down and I was quickly blocked again. Not that it made any difference. She very often used Tiffany and Tammie in her uploads, but there was never any sign of Skyla.

The deadline for the DNA results to be with the court was fast approaching and I had heard nothing. I was keen to know whether Ann had attended the doctor's surgery yet, so I gave them a call.

The receptionist was reluctant to tell me anything.

"I just want to know if the test has been done yet?" I argued.

"I can't divulge that" came the robotic response.

"Well," I said, gritting my teeth "I paid for the test and it's my daughter, so I think I have a right to know!"

"No, unless you have parental responsibility, I can't tell you anything".

I wondered if she had heard me right. Don't get me wrong, I knew what the issue was here. I knew that most DNA tests they were asked to do at the surgery would have been because a father was denying paternity.

"I DO have parental responsibility" I said, raising my voice a little.

"I am her father until proven otherwise, now has she had the test or not?". There was another nervous pause.

"Bear with me". She put me on hold and the call was then taken by a man.

"Hello, this is Dr Spencer, how can I help".

Fuck sake, I only wanted a simple bloody answer. I went through it again. I heard a rustling of paper and tapping of keyboard keys.

"No, Mr Organ", he said "she is booked to come in tomorrow".

My heart skipped a beat. "You have the letter I sent you, though don't you?" I said.

"I do" he replied.

"And you understand that I think she has been bringing her middle daughter to take the test and not Skyla?"

"Yes" he said quite softly. "Please don't worry, we have all of the paperwork here and the pictures that you sent with the letter".

"And you will take a picture won't you" I pressed.

"Yes" he said.

I breathed a sigh of relief. Soon I would have the results

Two days later I contacted the DNA company to make sure that they had received the tests back from the surgery and was disappointed to hear that they had not yet been returned. Time was really pressing on now and the constant feeling of panic that had become so normal for me now was getting worse. There were rumours from a couple of my friends who were still in contact with Ann that she was planning on moving to Devon to be with her boyfriend. I just had this feeling in the pit of my stomach that I couldn't shake. Was she planning on just running away with Skyla? She must know by now that I was never going to give up on my daughter.

I called the doctor surgery again to ask them if they had sent the tests back to the Surgery?
"No Mr Organ, Ann didn't attend the appointment".
"What?"
"Yes, we have contacted her and rearranged for this Thursday, she says that she forgot!".
That sick feeling intensified.

"What am I going to do" I asked miserably during a group video call.
"She can't just up and leave" said Nan "What about Tiffany's school?"
"Do you think Mike knows she might be leaving?" Rachel asked.

A new plan formed. We had no idea at this stage whether the rumours were true, but I wasn't going to sit back and let her disappear with my daughter. I realised that we would be able to use the law and court services to track her down, but that was going to take time. More time that I would be separated from Skyla, and I couldn't let that happen. Our focus on just getting a sighting of Skyla turned into watching Ann like a hawk and looking for clues that she might be moving.

Rachel contacted Mike's mother. Mike despised me so there was no point in me trying to contact him direct, but Rachel thought that a grandmother might have a bit of sympathy for me.

Rachel happily reported back that both Mike's mother and sister would do anything they could to keep us informed of any signs of Ann absconding. They had only just been allowed back into Tiffany and Tammie's lives and hated the thought of losing them again. Mike's mum explained how difficult it still was to see the girls.
"She won't allow him to see them on their own," she told Rachel. "She insists on being present at all times. Do you know how difficult it is to sit in a room and spend time with my grandchildren when that evil witch is in the room too and I have to make polite conversation? After all the lies she has told about Mike being violent, it's all I can do not to

throttle her," she said grimly.

"I can sympathise about the lies," I told Rachel, "but there was a restraining order against him, so he wasn't entirely innocent, was he?"

"His mum said that never happened! There has never been a restraining order. Yet another lie!" Rachel said bitterly.

I can't say I was ever going to become mates with Mike, but I did feel bad that I had believed everything she had said about him. As had half of Cirencester it seemed. The bloke had been labelled as a violent woman-beater who had a restraining order against him. We now knew that just wasn't true. Yet another of the fantasies that Ann had concocted to make herself appear to be the victim.

It was all about being the centre of attention with her. The lies, the stories, taking the kids to the hospital constantly for no reason at all! It was all about Ann making herself the centre of everybody's attention. Well, if I had my way, she would most definitely be the centre of attention once I proved what she had done.

The following Friday I contacted the doctors surgery yet again. At last, some positive news. Ann had brought Skyla to take the test and a courier had collected it to take back to the lab. Back to the waiting game.

The deadline for the results to be back didn't seem to matter anymore as the court date had now been set for the 2nd of October. That would be a full 8 months since I had seen Skyla.

This time, because I didn't have a solicitor, the results would go to Richard first and he would send them on. For the next few days, I resumed checking my phone every available opportunity, in anticipation for that all important email.

Finally, the results arrived on Friday 28th August. Again, I ignored the text in the email and the DNA test and scrolled frantically down to the picture. I didn't even look at the results at this stage, I just wanted to see a picture of Skyla.

And this time, if there had been even a shred of doubt in anyone's mind before, there it was. A large and very clear photograph of

TAMMIE. No head covering, but of a four-year-old child strapped into a pushchair. She had a surprised look on her face and her hair was standing on end, and I instinctively knew that this shot had been taken as a hat had been snatched from her head.

My heart sank. What the hell was I going to do now? There was no arguing with this picture, only I had nobody to argue for me anymore. A doctor had taken the sample from the wrong fucking child. How could this have happened? How could a doctor not know the difference between an 18th month old and nearly 4-year-old for Christ's sake?

I sent the results onto the group chat with a sad face emoji. I didn't have to wait long before almost simultaneously, Rachel, Dad, Mum, Nan, Jade typed 'Thats Tammie!!!'. To have them all ping up together gave the impression that the responses were being shouted, and I am almost sure they were.

Someone in the group started a video call but I ignored it. I couldn't face actually talking. It was all just too much. I was close to tears and felt closer to the edge than I had ever felt before. The judge had been very clear. "Final" DNA. Had this doctor just completely fucked up my life because he couldn't do one simple job?

"Join the call" Rachel typed into the group chat. What was the fucking point? I was never going to win. 3 times. 4 if you count the first DNA she had supposedly done with Dan. How did she have the balls to do it? To lie to the court. To lie to everyone. And why? What had I done to her that was so terrible that she would go to such extreme lengths to banish me from Skyla's life for ever?

I stared miserably at the photograph on my telephone screen, glancing briefly at the messages that were appearing from the group chat urging me to join the call. The last few were from Nan.

(Nan) We need to talk about what to do ned – we are waiting for you!

I really didn't want to add worrying about upsetting my nan to my list of things to feel miserable about, so I clicked on the button to join the video call.

"Come on now Carl" Rachel said sternly "Snap out of it, now is not the time to start feeling sorry for yourself".

"What can we do" I said angrily

"That is the clearest picture of Tammie we have ever had" Rachel said matter of factly, "so the first thing we do is write to the court and show them photos of Skyla to compare it to. It's a Bank Holiday weekend so we will get everything together over the next couple of days, OK?"

I looked up

"I suppose, but what if they don't believe me"

"We will MAKE them believe you" Nan said resolutely. "Contact Natalee and ask for a bit of advice. Tell her what has happened and tell her that you just need help and will pay:

Saturday morning was spent composing an email to Natalee that I hoped would show her that I wasn't stark raving bonkers.

'How do I get to speak to the judge and ask him to look at these photos' I asked.

Rachel was working hard on compiling images and putting them into an easy to view one-page document to show Natalee what we were trying to present to the court. She had laid the images out into sections. One line were images of all three children together, the second line was just of Tammie and the third was just of Skyla. One of the photos of Tammie was of course the photo that had been taken at the Doctors Surgery as identification for the DNA test. She marked this clearly so that any fool could see what we were talking about. Each photo was titled with the date but the big problem we had was that the only photos we had of Skyla were now nearly a year old.

There was no way Skyla could have changed THAT much, but considering a GP had failed to spot a near 4 year old girl being presented in place of an 18 month old, my faith in the system and people using their common sense was now practically nil.

My mum had a brainwave.

"Dan" she said. "He might have a more recent photo of Skyla".

I really didn't like the thought of involving him. I knew that he was as much of a victim in all this as me, but I still didn't like him much for sleeping with my girlfriend.

"Come on" Rachel agreed with Mum, "he probably didn't have a clue about you. The little spunk sponge probably cheated on you with countless blokes. It's not really his fault that he got mixed up in all of this".

I reluctantly agreed and Mum contacted him by instant message apologising for the intrusion but asking if he had a recent photograph of Skyla. I was sure he must have, but the thought of another man having more images of my baby girl than me really hurt. We waited anxiously for his reply but were a little taken aback to read the words 'can we meet?'

I really didn't know whether I liked that idea or not.

"Carl don't be stupid about it; I'll go and meet him and see what he has to say"

I glared

"He's probably just as confused and hurt as you are. That's if he even knows what's going on."

I knew she was right, but it didn't mean I was happy about it. Mum made the arrangements to meet Dan later that day.

When she got home, she presented me with two pictures of Skyla. I couldn't stop staring at them. She had changed so much and not at all! My heart ached as I gazed at her. In both photos she was being held by Ann and in one of them she had fresh tears under her eyes.

"Babies cry" Mum said.

I knew she was right, but it didn't make it any easier to see.

Mum told me about the meeting with Dan.

"He is just as broken as you" she said. "he said he doesn't believe he is her father. Says he tried, but just couldn't bond with her and stopped going round when Ann tried to get Tiffany to call him daddy".

What a bitch!

"He says that she would only let him see her if she was there too and was just weird – acting like they were a couple".

It didn't surprise me at all.

"Did you show him the picture of Tammie from the DNA test?"

"Yes – he says that's definitely Tammie"

OK, so I hadn't wanted to involve him, but at least I now had a couple more recent pictures of Skyla. I sent them onto Rachel to put into the document she was creating.

'Well at least something has gone my way I thought'. Later that Afternoon Mum and Dad went into town to do some shopping. They returned a couple of hours later with excited looks on their faces.

"What you so happy about?" I asked
"Look at this" said Dad
He passed me his phone and on it was a picture of Tammie, staring straight into the camera.
"Where did you get that?"
Dad started laughing. We were in Superdrug and Lynne was in there with Tiffany and Tammie.
"No Skyla?" I cut in
"No, just Tiffany and Tammie, anyway, Lynne didn't see us, and we were stood right behind them in the queue. Tammie kept turning around and smiling at me, she recognised me even with my mask on," he said proudly "so I just took a photo! By the time Lynne realised it was me and I had taken a photo it was too late"
"Did she not say anything?" I asked with a big grin on my face.
"Nope, just yanked her round so that she couldn't see us anymore and got out of there as fast as she could" he laughed.

The picture was perfect. It showed Tammie at her full height and there was no denying that this was the same child depicted in the DNA identification photograph. Another picture sent to Rachel for the "collage"

Tuesday morning came around and I sent the email with the images off to Natalee and crossed my fingers. If she didn't believe me, then there was no way I was going to be able to convince a judge!

I waited impatiently for a response but when it came, I was excited to read that she believed me. Somebody outside of my own family finally believed me and was able to give me a plan of action:

I was to email the court urgently and ask them to list it before a judge as this case was far too complex to be heard by a magistrate. She told me to do this as quickly as I could. She told me to include in the email a request for a further test that **must be** carried out in my presence along with a third party, such as a doctor so that there would be no risk of allegations being made against me. Or perhaps Dan would be prepared to be there bearing in mind that he would wish to know if he is actually the father or not too.

She also told me to ask the court to give a direction for me to file a statement with my exhibits and evidence.

I felt like I could breathe for the first time in weeks. I knew that she had doubted me before, but now she had seen those photos she was back on my side. I still had a mountain to climb, but I no longer felt that it was impossible.

My feelings of desperation and longing for this all to be over didn't ease while I waited for the court to respond to my request for a new date, but more importantly permission to file my evidence.

As procedure dictated, when I had sent my request to the court, I had sent a copy to Richard. I didn't hear anything for a couple of days, but I then received a copy of the email he had sent the court. In it he attached the latest DNA results along with a chain of emails between himself and the doctors surgery

Dear Dr Spencer
Before arrangements were made for this test, there was correspondence with the surgery, and we refer to the attached letter, which indicated that you would feel confident in recognising Skyla.

The importance of this issue was that Carl Organ who is currently named on Skyla's birth certificate as her father had disputed that previous samples had been taken from Skyla. Following this test, he is again saying that the sample was not taken from Skyla but was taken from her half-sister Tammie, born in 2017.
The purpose of requesting the sample be taken at the doctor's surgery by the doctor was hopefully to avoid any continuing issue about from which child the sample was taken. Are you able to declare that the sample was taken from Skyla rather than from Tammie?

I carried on reading through the chain. The doctor had responded:

Dear Richard

My secretary just passed on your most recent email. I have just spoken to Ms Carter, Ann's health visitor, about the situation we discussed last week.

Ms Carter knows the family well, and also did a video review with them last week. I asked her to look at the images I had taken of the child at the time of the DNA test.

Ms Carter confirmed that this was Skyla and not Tammie, as has been claimed by Mr Organ. She was 100% certain of this from the photograph and her knowledge of the family.

As per my letter, as I had only seen Skyla once before in December 2019, I was not 100% sure I could confidently claim the child the swab was taken from was Skyla, but following the discussion I had with Ms Carter today, I think we can be certain now

I hope this is some help.

My heart sank. Would the Court believe me over a doctor, a health visitor, a mother, and a solicitor?

"You have the photos" Rachel reminded me

I nodded, but knew they were useless if the court refused to see them. I still hadn't had a response to my request to file them and it was clear that her solicitor was pushing for them to refuse my request as he had written his own email to the court at the top of this email chain that said:

Further to the emails from Mr Organ to the court, please see the emails before from Dr Spencer.

We also attach the test results.

Contrary to what is alleged by Mr Organ the sample was taken from Skyla.

All I could do was wait. Finally, just 2 days later I received confirmation that my court date had been re-listed in the District Court on the 16th October. AND my request to submit evidence and a statement was also approved.

On the same day Dan's ex-partner, Sally, got in touch out of the blue. Dan had told her the whole sorry tale and she offered to help.

"I'm not sure you can" I said, "but thanks"

"I had a DNA test on Dan's son" she replied happily," I'll send you the results so you can see that Dan isn't a match. He can't be if the test is being done on Tammie".

As promised, she sent over the results. They looked like the DNA Legal results, but I didn't know how to read them or to use them as part of my evidence. I sent them over to Rachel, who spent the next few hours learning how to vaguely read DNA results.

Later she called me with excitement.

"This couldn't be more perfect" she said. "So, I've put it all in a document with the documents marked up, but basically, I've cross-matched Dan's DNA Markers from the test Ann said she had done and the test that Sally sent you.:

"And"

"Not the same bloke!" She said matter of factly. "I then checked the markers of Dan's **actual** test from Sally, against whatever child was tested in that very first test that she said she did and there is no way he can be the father."

"Also", she continued excitedly "Now that I understand how the DNA Markers work, I cross-matched the "Father" DNA to the "Child" DNA in that first test he thinks he took and even though it came back that he IS the father, he can't possibly be!" She exclaimed. "It's a fake! Without a doubt".

"How do you know?" I asked

"Right, it's difficult to explain but I'll try. The DNA tests over 20 different sets of 'markers'. Each marker has two numbers. The child will have one number taken from the mother and the other from the father. If only **one** of those markers doesn't share a number with the man tested, then he is **not** the biological Father" she explained.

I tried to keep up,

"And?"

"Well, on the results of that first test she did, there are **five** markers that show he cannot possibly be the father"

I silently tried to digest everything she was telling me.

"Look," she continued, "I've set it all out in a document and highlighted the markers that don't match for you to send with your evidence." She paused for a second and then said quietly

"We've got her Carl".

"Do you think?"

"Absolutely, if nothing else this proves she faked the first one. God, I hope they throw the book at her"

"Doubt it," I said bitterly "She's a woman with kids, seems like she can lie through her rotten front teeth, and nobody bats an eyelid." Just thinking about it made my temper flare "Be a whole different bloody story if it was a bloke though eh?"

Rachel sent me the new document and I put it together with the collage of photos. I was supposed to write a statement to go with it, but I had no idea where to start. As I sat there staring at the blank page on the computer my phone pinged to tell me there was a new message from Ashley.

I looked at the messages, feeling puzzled until I noticed that it was a chain of messages that had been between Ash and Mike!

(Ash) Can I ask you a question?
(Mike) *What?*
(Ash) *Is this Tammie?*

Ash had attached the last image from the doctor's surgery.

(Mike) I would say that's Tammie

Holy shit! It was like all the missing pieces of the jigsaw were finally coming together. Another bit of evidence to go to the court. Surely, they couldn't think I was some bloke completely off his nutter unable to accept the truth now. Not now that Tammie's own father had identified her.

"We should re-hire Natalee" my dad said. "I think we need to make sure this gets done right, and she will be able to help you with that statement."

The following day I put together all the evidence I had gathered and sent it to Natalee asking her to help again. As it was, she was already booked for my Court date, but she reassured me that she would find someone good to represent me.

I could start to relax a little. Someone who knew what she was doing had taken the reins again. I no longer had to go up against that smarmy piece of shit of a solicitor of hers. I knew that he was just doing what he was told by his "client", but he knew damned well that she had lied for her Legal Aid application. It really pissed me off that I was having to beg and borrow from my family to pay for all of this, when that lying little bitch got it all for free. British Justice? Whatever!

On the 14th of October Natalee sent me the statement that she and the barrister had compiled for the court to read. I was over the moon. It didn't take a genius to see that where Natalee had doubted me a few months earlier, now that she had seen the evidence, I had gathered any doubt was gone. Both she and my barrister had done a fantastic job of getting the strength of feeling across.

Where previously it had always been pitched as "I can't tell if that is Skyla", this statement most definitely stated "That is NOT Skyla, that is Tammie. Ann is committing fraud"

Some of the paragraphs had me practically punching the air. In the opening statement written on my behalf it said:

The entirety of these proceedings centres around 1 very important issue, namely, is the applicant of these proceedings the biological father of Skyla. F asserts that M has deliberately manipulated/ falsified or taken steps to affect the results to conclude that F is not the biological father. Each of the tests thus far will be covered in detail below.

The significance of this issue is so vast for all concerned and therefore careful consideration of all the evidence is needed.

It then went through the details of the case from start to finish. Outlining everything that had happened and why I believed that the first DNA test was fake, and the wrong child had been presented for all three legal DNA tests ordered by the court.

It finished the statement with:

Furthermore, if the outcome of said test shows that Skyla is the daughter of the applicant then there are going to be serious questions of the mother. We are talking above a potential change in residence, contempt of court and costs.

A potential change in residence? I didn't dare hope. But once I had proved that she was mine, I intended to fight tooth and nail to get custody. The shared custody arrangement was great a year ago, but after everything that had happened and the lengths, she had gone to keep me away from my little girl, there was no way in this world I could ever trust her. I would be forever wondering if she would be bringing her back each time or what lies she was concocting about me next. No. I couldn't risk it. Once I had the evidence that she was mine I would be applying for a 'Living with Order' and asking that contact with Ann be supervised contact only. That woman could not be trusted.

About an hour later I received the bundle. Jesus! The bundle contains all the documents and evidence for the case from start to finish. It contained a whopping 142 pages, but most importantly he had included all the evidence I had gathered. It included messages from both Mike and Dan identifying Tammie as the child in the DNA identification photographs in both the 2nd and 3rd court ordered DNA tests. I am pretty sure that was the most damning. Mike had everything to lose by assisting me, and as much as he hated me, he obviously felt he had to do the right thing. After all it was HIS daughter being used in this massive deception. I will be forever grateful to him for that.

My Position Statement and Bundle were all agreed and were sent to the court ahead of the hearing on the in just two days' time. A copy wen to Ann via her solicitor. I hoped she would see that the game was well and truly up when she saw everything laid out in front of her.

"She still might not be yours" Nan reminded me.

"She is" I said resolutely

Nan sighed. I understood what she was trying to say. It was clear that Tammie was being used to take the test in place of Skyla, but it was also clear that Ann had been less than faithful, so there was a possibility that Skyla wasn't mine after all.

"No," I said again, resolutely. "Skyla is mine."

And then came the final nail in Ann's coffin. I received a final email of the day from Natalee that made me literally clap my hands.

"What?" Nan said. She had just picked me up from work and was driving me home. I grinned at her. "Ann's solicitor has dumped her." I laughed.

I had no idea what had happened. It seemed very odd to me that just a short time after receiving all the paperwork for the hearing, suddenly, he was no longer acting for her. Things really were looking up.

After all this time of feeling like I was banging my head against a brick wall and shouting with nobody listening, things were starting to fall into place. I dared to hope.

The Hearing was very quick. Again, it was all done by telephone, so she really had no excuse. The court attempted to call her several times, but it just rang out. What was she up to now? Did she have another plan? Or was she just hiding now?

It went ahead in her absence, and I was over the moon when they agreed on yet another DNA test and that I should be present to identify Skyla myself. Now that Ann had no Solicitor, it also meant that she no longer had Legal Aid which meant her half of the cost of the DNA test wouldn't be covered. They discussed the cost being split between the two of us, but I really didn't want to give her any opportunity to delay any further and knew full well that she wouldn't pay her half. DNA Legal would not send the test kit until it had been paid for so I told them I would pay the full amount. Besides, once this mess was finally cleared up, I hoped that she would be ordered to pay my costs.

The court order was drawn up and this time it was ordered that the test should be conducted at the same Surgery that had messed up so badly last time, but that I would be present also. It also stated that Ann could take a companion. The results were ordered to be with the court by 4pm on the 16th of November.

This really was the final test. This one very clearly stated:

AND UPON the applicant agreeing that in the event that the DNA test results referred to at paragraph 8 below show that Carl Raymond Organ is not the biological father of Skyla Harris Organ the parties shall file an Order by consent for approval of the Court discharging the Child Arrangements Order dated 22nd January 2020 together with a Declaration that Carl Raymond Organ is not the biological father of Skyla Harris Organ and a request that the listed final hearing is vacated.

This was the fastest turnaround yet and I needed to get moving.

The first thing to do was to make the appointment at the doctors surgery, pay for the DNA test and get the kit sent there. Then we needed to notify Ann of the order. As she hadn't attended the hearing, she wouldn't know any of this and I didn't trust her not to say that she hadn't received her emails.

When the order came through from Natalee, she told me that she had sent it to Ann by email. But how would I know that she had got it?

Rachel contacted the doctors surgery and made the appointment. She did everything that was necessary at that end and then Nan contacted DNA Legal to give them the contact details of where to send the testing kit and make the payment. It was really turning into an 'all hands-on deck' event.

Rachel then typed up a letter to Ann informing her of the appointment time and reiterating that she MUST attend with Skyla. Dad printed the letter off twice and popped them into two separate envelopes along with a copy of the court order.

Next step, he hand delivered them. One copy to Ann's house and one copy to Lynne's house. We really were covering all bases. We knew that Ann stayed the night at her mums a lot and were determined not to give her any opportunity to say that she had never received it. Just to be sure, Dad filmed the delivery of both letters.

I was confident that we had done all we could, and things were going so well until DNA Legal contacted me to inform me that the doctors surgery had cancelled the appointment and informed them that they would not be hosting the test. I was angry, but Rachel was livid!
"How dare they?" she said. "It's a bloody court order. They can't just decide they aren't doing it"

She got on the phone straight away and asked to speak to the Practice Manager, Ms Adams. Rachel told me that it didn't go well. Ms Adams refused to budge and said she would not discuss it and hung up on her. This only succeeded in angering Rachel even more and so she jumped in the car and drove to the surgery from Swindon and demanded to see Ms Adams in person.

Rachel was very careful to remain as calm as possible, but she could clearly see that Ms Adams was not happy for her to be there, even threatening to call the police. "Please do," Rachel said, "I just need you to see how important this is and want you to help us fix YOUR mistake". Eventually a senior Dr was called, and he allowed Rachel to go through the whole sorry tale, where she ended up breaking down with sheer frustration that we had seemed to be getting closer to the end of this horrendous ordeal only to be blocked again. After a long argument and pointing out the court order, the Surgery reluctantly reinstated the appointment.

Everything was back on track and DNA Legal confirmed that the courier had been arranged to deliver the test in plenty of time for the appointment that had been arranged for that Friday at 4:00pm

Friday came around and it felt like time had come to a standstill again. Then at 3:00pm I received a message from Natalee. Ann had sent an email to Natalee telling her that she couldn't make the appointment and could we please arrange it for another time.

Natalee had responded with a very curt "you must attend" listing the repercussions for defying a Court Order, but she hadn't heard anything since. Another blow,
"Maybe she will turn up?" Rachel said. "Natalee has told her she will be in contempt of court if she doesn't, so maybe that will frighten her into going"
It was a faint hope, but it was all I had. Rachel drove me to the surgery, and I went into Reception to let them know that I had arrived for the appointment. COVID restrictions meant that there was no waiting room access and so I returned to sit in the car and wait. 4:00pm came and went and there was no sign of Ann. Yet again, my heart sank as I realised she wasn't coming.

At 4:30 I returned to the reception desk and told them I was giving up. I was devastated. I was so close to the truth. Why couldn't she just give up and have Skyla take the test?

"I've spoken to your barrister" Natalee said, "he says to rearrange the appointment and I will write to her and warn her that if she fails to comply, we will make an application to have her committed to prison for being in contempt of court".

This raised my spirits a little. Surely this would frighten her enough to make her comply.

And then Ms Adams from the doctors surgery took it upon herself to write to Natalee and tell her that because Ann had failed to attend her appointment the surgery did not feel that they could offer another. Particularly as they were already overstretched in the middle of a National Pandemic.

I was furious that she had written to my solicitor without my consent. Money was tight and this was costing me and my family a fortune without overpaid receptionists taking it upon themselves to add to my bill. But I also understood that Ann had given them the perfect excuse to refuse to host the test. They had never wanted to do it in the first place. But I was also puzzled as to why they weren't taking this perfect opportunity to fix the almighty fuck up they had made by identifying the wrong child. But then I supposed, they didn't believe they HAD made a mistake. After all, Ms Carter had confirmed the child was Skyla.

Now we had a race to find another venue. Natalee offered her office, but that would be billed to me and it was in Swindon. The distance would be a perfect excuse not to attend.

Yet again, Rachel sprang into action. She contacted our own surgery in Cirencester. Our whole family has always had a great relationship with this particular surgery and thankfully they agreed to host the test, although we would have to pay for it. I figured it was still going to be a hell of a lot cheaper than at Natalee's office, so we gratefully made the appointment.

Natalee had to contact the court and ask for an amendment to the order. There was no point just asking Ann to attend the new location. She was so desperate not to go for the test it stood to reason that she would argue that she couldn't be forced to do anything outside of the order. So more unnecessary expense.

The bill was well over £7,000 at this point and still rising. Still, it had to be done. The new order was raised and DNA Legal arranged to send a new kit to the surgery. Again, we composed letters for Ann to inform her of the new appointment and again we delivered them by hand.

One day before the appointment Natalee contacted me. She was slightly bemused but felt that she should inform me that Sandra from the Churn Project had contacted her to make sure that I would turn up to the appointment.
"I beg your pardon?"
"I know" said Natalee
"Checking that I turn up"? I said emphasising the 'I'
"Yep"
"What did you tell her"
"I told her I couldn't discuss my client with her"

Fuck sake. I didn't care that Sandra was sticking her nose in again, but I did care that she had just upped my legal fees again. Who the hell did she think she was? There was nothing I could do about it now except write a 'snot-'o'gram' telling her that she had no business contacting my legal representative and elevating my costs.

The appointment day came, and I checked my phone constantly to make sure that she Ann hadn't come up with some lame excuse, but all remained quiet.

Rachel came to collect me to take me to the surgery in plenty of time.
"Just in case she tries to pull a fast one by getting there early and leaving before you arrive" she explained.
Covering all bases again. Leaving nothing to chance.
We arrived at the surgery and let the receptionist know we were there and then returned to the car to wait. Sitting in silence and turning to look at every car that pulled into the car park, straining to see if Ann was in the vehicle.

Finally, a car pulled into the carpark. Sandra from the Churn project was driving the car. I recognised her from their website.

"Come on," said Rachel, opening the car door and getting out. "We may as well go in now."

We both pulled on our face masks that were now mandatory in all indoor spaces to help stop the spread of COVID.

I don't think I have ever felt more nervous. I wanted to stare into the car to see if I could see Skyla but forced myself to keep my eyes forward as I walked past and headed to the surgery reception.

Rachel and I were directed to the waiting room where we took a seat. And then got up and paced, and then sat, and then paced. Where were they? What were they doing?

Finally, we heard voices in Reception.

"She doesn't want to wait in the waiting room, she's feeling very nervous" I heard Sandra say

I couldn't hear what the receptionist said in response.

"Is that woman with Carl?"

Rachel had stood up again and was visible from reception through the waiting room door.

Again, I couldn't hear the response.

The waiting room was a large, almost circular room with the doctors' offices to the right. There was no way of accessing the surgeries without going through the waiting room. The door to my right opened and a nurse came through and headed towards the door to reception.

The nurse opened the door,

"Come through" she said

With that Ann came into view in the waiting room holding a child. She was covering the child's head with her hand but at the same time, covering her own face by keeping it as low as possible and pressed into the child.

She rushed through and headed straight to the far door and the doctors' offices with Sandra following closely behind.

Both myself and Rachel got up to follow them and Sandra turned as though to stop Rachel.

"What are you doing?" She asked Sandra

Sandra looked confused.

"Don't think for one second that Ann is going in there with you, and Carl goes in alone" she said quite aggressively,

The Nurse turned back and held her hands out.

"Just Ann and Skyla for now" she said calmly.

Rachel walked towards the nurse

"The court order states that Carl has to identify Skyla" she explained.

The nurse took the order and put her hand on my arm. Give me five minutes she said softly. She directed Ann towards an office and as Sandra made to follow, Rachel blocked her.

Sandra looked uncomfortable.

"Is that Skyla she has with her?" Rachel asked?

"Yes"

"How the hell can you offer so much support to her after what she has done?"

"She hasn't done anything" Sandra said

"Really? Have you ever met Tammie?"

"Yes"

Rachel started going through the folder we had brought with us. She pulled out the picture of Tammie that had been taken during the last DNA test at the previous Surgery.

"This," said Rachel "is the child that Ann said was Skyla for the last DNA test"

Rachel held out the piece of paper

"I haven't got my glasses on"

Rachel laughed "It's OK, I printed it really big for you!"

Rachel continued to hold the picture in front of her until Sandra lifted her eyes to glance at the image. Her eyes widened and she quickly looked behind her as though looking for a seat.

"Well, I'm just here to support Ann" she replied

"Shame you don't offer support to the victim in all this" Rachel snapped.

Sandra was starting to look uncomfortable and turned and headed towards a seat facing the doorway that Ann had just gone through.

I didn't have to wait long, the door opened, and the nurse poked her head round and beckoned me over.

My heart was in my mouth as I followed her to a small room. I could see the back of Ann's head. She was still playing the role of victim.
"Give that girl an Oscar" I muttered under my breath as I watched her cower away as I entered the room.

The child was still being held tightly in her arms with her face turned away from me and that bloody pink woolly hat fixed firmly to her head when the Nurse pointed at her and said calmly
"Can you confirm this is Skyla?"
"I can't see her face" I replied
The nurse motioned to Ann to turn herself around so that the child was more clearly visible to me. Ann shifted the weight of the child so that she was more visible whilst ensuring that she didn't have to meet my gaze for even a second.
"Can you take the hat off?"
Ann lifted her hand and snatched the hat off the child's head as though my request was entirely unreasonable.

And there she was. My Skyla.
"Wow, all that hair she grew for those DNA tests has gone," I said sarcastically.
Skyla had a little more visible hair than she had the last time I had seen her, but the thick fringe of the child pictured in all three DNA identification photos was non-existent.

"Is that Skyla?" the Nurse asked again
I nodded in response not trusting myself to talk any more. Skyla had started to cry, clearly upset by the tension in the room. I couldn't even take my mask off. I felt sure that if she could see my face, she would recognise me, and my presence would make her less frightened.

Finally, Skyla was going to be taking the DNA test.
"You are happy for the sampling to go ahead?" the Nurse said smiling.

I smiled back at her forgetting that I had this blasted mask on. I followed it with a nod, scared to speak in case my voice cracked. The last thing I wanted to do was cry in front of that bitch.

DNA Legal had insisted that another sample be taken from me as it had been so long since the last one. The cynical side of me thought that it was because I had to cover the cost of the entire test this time and testing the sample from me as well would bump up the price. DNA doesn't bloody change. Still, I suppose it meant that Ann couldn't suddenly decide that the DNA that had been analysed against Skyla's wasn't mine! I would put nothing past her.

I moved to a different room to have my sample taken from a doctor and then left the surgery through the back door following the one-way system.

Climbing back into the car I could feel myself welling up again. It was a mixture of utter devastation that Skyla had looked so frightened and hadn't recognised me and relief that soon this would all be over. Or would it? Once I had the results and she could no longer deny what I had known all along, would the shared custody arrangement be reinstated. I had to be prepared for the fact that the court might feel that I needed to be reintroduced to Skyla slowly, after all, I had been missing from her life for the best part of a year now.

It didn't seem fair. After the monumental fight I had put up, they still might only allow me to see her in a contact centre. I tried not to think about it. The important thing was that I would soon be able to prove to the world that Ann was a lying bitch who had lied to not only me but so many other people.

I returned home to play yet another waiting game. This one was set to be the shortest but still felt like another lifetime.

The next few days dragged by so slowly as I returned to the now established habit of checking my phone for new emails at every available opportunity. This time, because I had paid for the entire test, the results would come direct to me with a copy being sent to Natalee and Ann by email.

This time the results took longer. Mixed with confusion over when couriers would collect the sample and then missing the deadline to get the samples into the analysis process before the cut-off time all contributed to further delays. I felt like the whole universe was conspiring to make this ordeal last for as long as humanly possible.

Until finally, on Thursday 19th November at 3:30pm, I saw it in my mailbox. My hands started to shake as I tapped the screen to open the email, then the enclosed attachment.

This was it. It had to be it. Skyla had definitely had the test; I had been there! I swallowed hard as my phone opened the PDF attachment. From previous experiences of receiving these reports, I now knew how far to scroll down to get to the important part.

The now familiar table with columns containing the DNA Marker figures of both myself and, this time, Skyla, side by side. My eyes searched for the bottom of the table and that all important sentence that gave the scientific conclusion of the report.

I read the words

'CONCLUSION:
Based on our analysis and the biostatistical evaluation of the results, it is practically proven that Carl Raymond Organ is the biological father of Skyla Harris Organ'.

I read the words again. "IS", "IS". My eyes flicked up to the paragraph above

'The probability of Carl Raymond Organ being the biological father of Skyla Harris Organ is 99.9995 %'

At that moment I literally didn't know what to do with myself. I found that I was holding my breath and tears were burning my eyes. It was over. I could wave this precious piece of paper right under the noses of all those doubters. This was proof that I was not mad. It was proof that Ann was as evil as I had told everyone she was. Proof that the health visitor, the doctor, her solicitor had all been conned.

I knew that my entire family were waiting just as anxiously as I had been. I opened our group chat and selected the video call.

Rachel was first to answer. I did my best to keep a neutral expression on my face while we waited for others to join us.
"Are the results in?" Rachel asked half excitedly and half nervously
I nodded
"And?" I tried to look miserable but in my current mood that was an impossible task. I was trying hard to delay blurting it out until everyone had joined the call.
"She's yours, isn't she?" Rachel said matter of factly
Again, I tried to keep a straight face but couldn't contain myself any longer and broke into the grin that would not be contained a second longer
"Oh my GOD" Shouted Rachel as she leapt from her chair and kind of started pacing the room. It was clear that her excitement would not allow her to stay seated.
She turned back to the camera, and I could see tears in her eyes too
"Oh Carl, I can't believe it. It's finally over"
"What? What? What's going on? Have you got the results?" Nan had joined the conversation but was obviously driving so was on hands-free with only sound.
I started laughing.
"She's mine".
"What". Nan shouted, "I can't hear you Carl". I could hear her muttering under her breath as the signal faded in and out and she was only hearing parts of the conversation.
"SHE'S MINE" I said loudly
At that moment Mum, Jade and Ashley had all joined the call.

I couldn't help but feel overwhelmed as everyone was shouting their congratulations.

"Got to go" I declared. "I need to call Natalee!"

I left the video call and got straight onto the phone to Natalee. She had already read the results and was quick to congratulate me.

"Well," she said, "you got there in the end".
"What now?" I said, keen to get to the matter of organising access to my daughter.
"Well, I will write to Ann and ask her to reinstate the shared custody arrangement immediately. I've looked at the dates and according to the original schedule you should have Skyla on Tuesday. That would give Ann the chance to read the results and consider a response over the weekend".
"I want to go and get her right now." I stated.
"Not a good idea" Natalee said firmly. "You've come too far to give her a reason to accuse you of assault or something worse at this stage" she continued.
I knew she was right, but Tuesday seemed so far away.
"Do you think she will agree?" I questioned
"I don't know, but she knows she is in a lot of trouble now, so maybe she will start to cooperate in the hope that it will look better for her in court"
I really hoped so.
"I'll also make an application for an urgent hearing" she finished

I left Natalee to contact Ann by email with her suggestion. It was now coming up to 5:00pm so I knew that I wouldn't be hearing anything tonight.

That night was the happiest I had felt in a very long time. The night was spent daydreaming about the things I would be doing with Skyla in just a few days' time. The places I would take her, the games I would play with her. I kept telling myself that it might not happen as quickly as next week to try and contain my own disappointment if Ann stayed true to form and deliberately obstructed me, but my excitement was just too much to keep in check.

I couldn't help but shout my excitement as a Facebook status. *"Best news of my life – I'm Skyla's Dad!!!"* I announced to the world.

I spent the rest of the night reading the many messages of support that I received as both comments on my status update and in the private messages I received. It was good to know that so many people were happy for me.

Most surprising of all was the number of Ann's friends who contacted me offering their congratulations and apologies for the way they had treated me. Her former best friend was racked with guilt for having been so stupid as to believe every word that Ann had told them. Of course, I had no bad feeling towards any of them. Ann had perfected the act; I couldn't blame them for believing her. I mean, faking DNA tests was pretty ballsy, and I don't think any of her friends ever believed that she was capable of it.

I didn't believe that she was capable of it on her own. I couldn't tell you for sure who was helping her, but I was damn sure she hadn't gone through with it all without support from someone and the most likely would have been the woman who hated me possibly more than Ann herself did! Her Mother.

Friday arrived and it was hard not to keep checking my mail and messages, but lunch time delivered the sweetest present I could have wished for.

Not only had Ann agreed to reinstate the shared custody arrangements she had stated in her email to Natalee that I could collect Skyla from her mother's house at 2:00pm on Sunday.

I hadn't dared hope for such an outcome. I was still waiting for confirmation of when I should return her. Picking her up on Sunday meant we were outside of the schedule and the last thing I wanted was to give her an excuse to make trouble for me because I had failed to adhere to the agreement. Natalee had replied to her email asking for clarification but had heard nothing back.

It was now 4:30pm on a Friday and Natalee was tidying up loose ends before shutting up shop for the weekend.

"I've sent her another email asking her to confirm when she expects Skyla to be returned and to which address" she told me, "But if she doesn't reply, I suggest you go on Sunday to collect Skyla and we will chase again on Monday".

It sounded good to me, but I was incredibly nervous about what Ann might be up to. The most obvious conclusion was that as soon as I had Skyla for a few hours I would receive a call from the police accusing me of abduction or something just as nasty. It made me nervous as essentially Ann had a court order that prevented me from having contact with Skyla until paternity had been established.

We had yet to present the results to the court which meant that if the police did call, despite having the evidence to prove I was her father, the court order might still be accepted as evidence that I should have no contact with her. It would be the weekend and so Natalee wouldn't be able to explain for me and they might take her from me and maybe even arrest me for abduction or something until it could all be sorted out when Natalee returned to work on Monday.

Still, nothing was going to stop me going to get her at 2:00pm on Sunday.

Saturday was spent preparing her room. Mum and Dad were as excited as I were and as a family, we put her cot back together. It was the cot that I had purchased second-hand back in December when this whole nightmare had started. I had reluctantly dismantled it and put it out of sight in around May. Seeing it had just been too painful and a constant reminder of what I had lost.

This time we turned Ashley's old bedroom into Skyla's room. I wanted to purchase a few outfits for her, but of course, I didn't even know what size she was wearing now. There was so much that I didn't know about my little girl. She had just started crawling when I last saw her, but was she talking yet? Mia, her cousin was just starting to form words so it stood to reason that Skyla might be too. What did she like to eat? Did she have any allergies? What did she like to do? Play with?

It broke my heart to realise that I didn't know her at all anymore. Would she remember me? Would she want to be with me? I don't think I could bear it if she was scared of me. She had seemed scared in the doctors surgery during the DNA test, but I hoped that was because of the tense atmosphere. I prayed she would recognise me as soon as she saw me without the mask.

Sunday arrived after a sleepless Saturday night, and I watched the clock tick slowly around to 1:30pm. I started to pull on my coat and shoes. I was ready. I had put the child seat in the car ready to drive her home.

Dad got behind the wheel and Mum in the passenger seat. I sat in the back next to the empty child seat. The short drive to Lynne's house seemed to take forever, but also went too fast. We were about 10 minutes too early. We pulled up outside the house and I waited watching the clock tick over minute by long minute.

The second it ticked over to 2:00pm I jumped out of the car and headed down the path. I took a deep breath and tapped on the door sharply with my bare knuckles.

I could hear a child crying from within the house. The door swung open, and I looked up to see Ann holding a crying Skyla. She didn't even look at me. I don't know what I had expected, but what happened next was beyond belief. Not one word was spoken as she literally thrust Skyla at me. I put my arms out to take her from her and I had barely finished wrapping my arms around her before the door was slammed shut.

I could do nothing else but turn and take Skyla to the waiting car and strap her in. Skyla was beside herself. I ran round the car and jumped into the seat next to her. Mum and Dad were turned in their front seats trying to soothe her.

"Let's just get her home" I said hopeful that she would settle once we got her there.

I put my hand out to Skyla to reassure her and her little hand grabbed hold of it. And held on tight.

Dad drove us home and I got her out of the car and into the house. Every time I took my hand away from hers, she cried even harder. I sat in the armchair holding onto her as tightly as she was holding onto my hand.

This is how she stayed for the next hour. She had stopped crying, but any attempt made to move her to remove her coat resulted in more tears. Mum and Dad made attempts to distract her with toys, bottles, and food but there was no moving her.

She seemed very sleepy, and I waited patiently as she drifted into a sleep. Carefully I removed her coat and made myself comfortable. I sat there staring at her as she slept. Her eyes red and puffy from crying. She looked and sounded like she had a cold and had a nasty cough that made her stir from her sleep often. It sounded terrible but I couldn't give her any Calpol to help as I had no idea if she had been medicated at Ann's. I suspected that she had been as that would explain her sleepiness.

I couldn't take my eyes off her. Here she was. Finally, my princess was back where she belonged. In my arms. I held her as tightly as she held me. I never wanted to let her go again.

She slept for a couple of hours and as she started to wake, I braced myself for more tears as she tried to comprehend where she was. To my surprise and delight, she peered at me, still gripping my hand, and smiled.

With her free hand she reached up and put her fingers in my beard. I grinned broadly as she continued to stare and smile at me.
"She remembers me, I'm sure of it" I said happily to Mum and Dad
"I think she does" Mum replied

Over the next couple of hours, I savoured every moment with this precious girl. Soaking in all up and trying to commit everything to memory. All the while waiting for the expected knock at the door from the police, come to take her "home". But it didn't come.

Skyla settled in beautifully and surprised us all with her expert use of a mobile phone. She knew exactly how it worked and was obsessed with You Tube.

"It's easy to see how she has been entertained over the last year" Mum said grimly

"I'm surprised Ann tore herself away from it long enough to let Ann play with it" I retorted but it was clear to see that Skyla had most certainly spent more than the recommended amount of time staring at a mobile telephone screen.

Later that evening, I carried Skyla up the stairs to settler her into her cot. I was expecting her to be upset at being settled for the night in a "strange" room but again she surprised me. If she was missing her Mum and Sisters, she certainly didn't show it.

Unsurprisingly Skyla didn't sleep through the night. Most parents of small children dream of a full night's sleep with no disturbance, but I can honestly tell you that being woken that night to the sound of my baby crying was amazing. Obviously, I didn't want her to be upset for any reason at all, but the sound of her cry was a million times sweeter than not having her near me at all.

I dived out of my own bed to comfort my girl. Again, rather than being upset at seeing a "strange" man instead of her mother, I was greeted with a beautiful smile.

Monday the 23rd of November arrived, and I was still none the wiser as to when Ann wanted me to bring Skyla back. That was soon to be answered when I received the next email from Natalee

She had received an email with a letter attached from Ann. The message in the email body text read:

Dear Natalee

Please see attached a letter for yourself and your client Mr Carl Organ and the family court, in response to this letter this is to be kept personal between Mr Carl Organ himself, yourself and the family court only please.

I was intrigued and opened the attachment. What I read next left me lost for words.

To whom it may concern,

In light of recent event of what's happened I feel as a mother to my other children I feel the setup of the court order it would not benefit Skyla's best interest or to my other children for a settled household .I have thought long and hard about the decisions for Skyla's best interest and have come to a conclusion that I would be willing to hand over all parental rights to Mr carl organ (father).Due to circumstances which I will not go into at this time as it of a personal matter .Therefore I think in Skyla best interest she would be better off staying in one household rather than being shuffled household to household every couple of days in relation to the court order .

As of Sunday 22nd November 2020, I hand over full parental rights to Mr carl organ on the terms he does not post it on social media or post this information anywhere else or disclose within anyone beset himself and the courts.

Also, I request that all his friends and family do not contact me.

I will sign any documents needed for this if sent direct by email only.

I couldn't believe what I was reading. How could she? After all this. All the lies to force me out of her life she was handing her over and wanted no further contact with her?

What the hell had the last year been about? It certainly hadn't been about Skyla. "How could she" I said repeatedly to myself.

Yesterday she had shoved her at me like she was nothing more than a bag of rubbish and slammed the door. She had known that she wasn't coming home, and she hadn't even so much as given her a kind word. A goodbye. A kiss. Nothing. And what about her things?

She had sent her away with none of her possessions. She had no comforter, no bottle and certainly no change of clothes. I could, and most certainly would provide Skyla with absolutely everything she needed but couldn't get my head around the fact that her mother hadn't even cared enough to send her away with something familiar to cling to. Her selfishness and evil really knew no bounds.

Over the next few days, I got to know my daughter all over again. And every moment filled me with joy. I tried to forget about Ann for now, but my anger was triggered again when during that week I was sent image after image of adverts that Ann was posting on Facebook Marketplace. She was having a mass clear-out. Every item that had belonged to Skyla was now listed for sale. All her toys, her bed, everything. There it all was for the highest bidder to purchase. She was erasing Skyla from her life.

Again, her profile had been changed as had her mothers. Ann's bio listed just Tiffany and Tammie as did Lynne's. Skyla was nothing to them anymore.

I can't say I was upset at the thought of never having to fight to see her again, but what about Skyla? What about what she might want? I hated Ann, but she was still Skyla's mother.

Consequences

The court date had been set for the 17th of December. I doubted that Ann would turn up for fear of the consequence of her actions.

"She must be shitting herself" everyone said. I had no doubt that she wouldn't be sent to prison or anything, but there must be some consequences for her actions.

On the 17th of December I dialled in to the hearing and was surprised that Ann had dialled in as well. I won't deny, my heart sank a little. Was she going to be asking for contact? Shared custody? I seriously hoped not, and if she was, I was going to beg for Supervised contact only. She really couldn't be trusted. And after that letter she had sent saying it wasn't in Skyla's best interest to go between the two homes, I hoped they would see how callous she had been.

"They might just see it as a knee-jerk reaction from a scared woman." Nan said bitterly
"Yep, playing the victim again." I agreed

But again, she surprised us. I had given up trying to work her out. This time she had gone all the way. This time Ann had applied to the court to relinquish her parental responsibility.

On one hand I felt relieved that I would never have to deal with that bitch again, but on the other just so very sad for my daughter. She was going to grow up without a mummy. OK Ann was a lousy mother and a terrible role-model for any child, but still? How is Skyla going to feel in years to come knowing that her mother didn't want anything to do with her?

Trying to force me out of her life and pretending another man was her father was bad enough, but to willingly walk out of her life? I couldn't comprehend it.

The judge was clearly as shocked by the application as I was, insisting that she speak alone with Ann. I assume to ensure that she wasn't being bullied into making such a drastic approach, but Ann was adamant.

She was even offered time to consider her options and set a new court date. Another suggestion she rejected.

Ultimately the court rejected the application as to allow it would have meant that Ann would not be responsible for paying maintenance for her daughter, but it was ordered that Skyla would reside with me and no order for contact was made for her mother.

I now had sole custody and I was on top of the world. For about 2 minutes.

"Hang on a minute" I thought. Is nobody going to address the fact that she has lied and cheated all this time? Apparently not. I was livid, there was not even a mention of it. How could she do all that, commit fraud, cost the tax-payer shit loads of money and nobody was even going to ask her why she did it?

The closest I got to any form of justice was in the form of costs, and even that came nowhere near the nearly £10,000 it had cost me to fight her lies.

Because she had received Legal Aid for the vast majority of the case, she could not be asked to pay any contribution to my costs for that period. She was only ordered to pay for my costs from the moment her Solicitor had dumped her. Just £5,500 of it. I was fuming. Legal Aid may have picked up the bill for HER costs, but why wasn't she made to pay all of mine? I had been forced to pay massive fees solely because of her lies and deceit. The law really is an ass.

Still, I consoled myself. It really was over. I could now look forward to the rest of my life with Skyla. It was tough. I had to start from scratch, but every moment with my little girl was worth it.

I was still seething at the part that the doctor and the health visitor had played in identifying the wrong child.

I compiled letters of complaint outlining everything that had happened and enclosing all the evidence that had been sent to the court.

I needed answers. Their "Expert" testimony could have cost me my daughter and they needed to know the implications of what they had done.

The doctors surgery launched a full investigation, and I must confess, despite my anger at the time, their long-awaited response to my complaint included a full and frank disclosure of their investigations. Along with a genuine apology, they outlined the lessons learned from the incident. The complaint about Ms Carter, however, was taking a lot longer.

In the meantime, I was offered a flat. It was perfect. It needed some work doing to it before I could move in, but again my family were there to help. My dad spent countless hours helping me decorate. I relished every moment of decorating Skyla's room. A pink room fit for a princess.

We moved into our new home after Christmas and spent the next few months creating the most fantastic bond.

During this time the visits, and what I now perceived to be interference, from health visitors increased. I realised that they saw me as "obstructive", but they were clearly still of the opinion that Skyla should be with her mother. On one occasion in February of 2021, the health visitor at that time even asked if she could share my address with Ann as she had a right to know where her daughter was and looked shocked when I refused. It was clear from the way that she was talking that Ann was continuing to play her role as victim when talking to the health department. Rather than admit that she had abandoned her daughter, it was evident that she was behaving as though she was trying everything in her power to receive even a snippet of news about her daughter. Was this because she was ashamed of what she had done and didn't dare admit it to health professionals? Or because to continue her victim act fulfilled her need for attention? I didn't know, but what I did know was that the continued aggressive pushing for a "relationship" to be maintained with her maternal family was really starting to get on my nerves.

Why couldn't they understand that it was Ann that had cut all contact with Skyla? I was the bloody victim here. Me and Skyla.

The complaint to the NHS Trust regarding Ms Carter having identified the wrong child was still in the investigation stages, but in the meantime, I decided to make a Freedom of Information Request to obtain the health visitor records for Skyla.

"At least then I will know what she has said about me in all this," I reasoned to Mum "she is obviously telling them a pack of lies".

These things take time, but when the file finally came through, it was interesting to read their defensive response in their covering letter.

We are aware that you may not agree with all the information contained within the record, the health visitor had reported what she was told at the time.

I sat down with a cup of coffee and braced myself for some unpleasant reading and a whole new set of lies and fabrications made up by Ann and I certainly wasn't wrong.

It took me days to compile my response to them applying to utilise my rights to have the records amended to reflect the truth.

Skyla's health visitor records were just filled with Ann's lies but what upset me most was the fact that literally everything she told them was recorded and written in these reports as though they were truth.

For example, back in the November of 2019 when Skyla was first living with me at my parents when this whole nightmare first started, the health visitor had written

Known to have assaulted family member, health visitor not willing to attend as lone worker

As I read through the documents, I could match Ann's behaviours with what was happening during the court process.

On 1st July, because of the request for Ms Carter to be a witness to the DNA testing, it is mentioned in the report:

Current situation is that Skyla is now living with Ann. Skyla has now had 3 DNA tests to establish who her father is. The results have shown that Carl Organ is not the father, however, Carl Organ is claiming that one of Ann's other children had been tested instead. The judge has ordered a 4th test with a witness present from the Health Visiting Team.

The next day they left a message for Ann to contact them and recorded on the 3rd of July:

Mother reports that Skyla is now in her care but is meant to be having planned supervised contact with her father, Carl Organ.

Another lie. At that time, she was claiming to the court that Dan was Skyla's father and there was no provision for me to have any contact at all.

The most telling though, was the switch in how Ann was reported to be responding in the health visitor reports as time progressed. She had gone from 'no issues here' from February to September to a new 'victim' role in October. Suddenly, the reports show that Ann is now claiming that she is struggling to bond with Skyla and blaming the 2 months separation. Although she was now claiming it was 5 months! It doesn't take a genius to figure out that she realised that her lies were about to be exposed and so she was forming a whole new back-story to excuse her past behaviour and a reason for giving Skyla up.

I could feel my anger rising again as I read through all the lies that had been recorded in the notes that nobody ever seemed to question, and yet absolutely nothing about the huge deception and the web of lies is mentioned in there. No wonder I always felt like I was being judged by health visitors. I most definitely was! If I had read all of that about me without knowing what really happened, I would think I was an asshole too!

After reading the health department records, I am doing everything in my power to make sure that the truth is recorded correctly where necessary. I can't spend the rest of my life wondering if Skyla's future teachers, doctors or anybody else who have a vested interest in her health and development think I am a terrible person who hits children and women and deprives a mother of her child.

But having said that I have also decided that it is most definitely time to move on with my life. This whole episode taught me one very important lesson. I can achieve anything with the love and support of my family behind me and beside me, and now I was ready to throw myself into being a single, full time daddy.

Watching her grow and achieve life's milestones are everything I live for. It would be so easy to stay resentful of everything I missed, but what would be the point of that? I missed her first words, her first steps and I am sure many other things, but I am going to be there for every important event going forward.

She loves spending time with her cousin, and I am so grateful that they are so close in age. I am confident that their bond will be unbreakable. Someone she can share all of life's milestones with. I am ready for everything life throws at us. I survived the last year and the evil that Ann put me through so I don't think there is anything I can't withstand. With Skyla to fight for, there is little I can't achieve.

Of course, there are parts of an adolescent girl's development that are going to be challenging for the pair of us, but I hope that her relationship with Mia will mean a close bond with her Aunt Jade. I am sure that Aunt Jade will include Skyla in those important "girly" chats that she has with Mia as she grows into a young woman. It will certainly be less of an embarrassment for her than me attempting it. But attempt it I will if that's what is needed.

I have yet to decide how I am going to handle the questions about her mother. It's going to be difficult for both of us. She won't be ready for this book until she is a lot older. The truth is far too brutal for a child. I am going to have to find a healthy balance between the truth and not leaving her with feelings of abandonment.

But I do promise to tell her the truth, I just need to find a sensitive way of telling it. But there is time. Those questions are a few years away yet, and when they come, I will be ready with my truthful answers.

2020 was the year from hell and I wouldn't wish what I went through on my worst enemy (except maybe Ann), but it most definitely proved to me that I am stronger than I ever thought possible.

Here's to 2021 and beyond. The future is bright.

Printed in Great Britain
by Amazon

69501821R00078